Usury: Money from Nothing Leaving Debt for Thee

J. F. Scarbrough

Table of Contents

Dedication Page

To the Audit Services Philosophers' Roundtable - where it all began.

1. Pick Up and Write

"So too let him rejoice and delight in finding you who are beyond discovery rather than fail to find you by supposing you to be discoverable" - St. Augustine[1]

July 5th, 2016. I can still vividly remember the day. From the outside looking in, it must've looked like nothing consequential, but this day changed the entire course of my life and thereafter. Just a few days prior, I was completely uncertain of whether God existed, but after July 5th, 2016, there was simply too much evidence for me to doubt anymore.

Around 9:30 that morning, sheer euphoria rushed over me like I've never felt before and previously bewildering questions now seemed like the most obvious truths. I had spent years racking my brain on the perennial questions one has when doubting religion - "If God is all good and all powerful, then why is there evil in the world?" "With so many religions out there, how can just one claim to be true?" "How can I know!?"

And then – poof - all the doubt was eviscerated. Once you know who Keyser Söze is or why Bruce Willis never opens doors in the *Sixth Sense*, you can never watch those movies the same way again. The truth is staring you right in the face! Much like the revelation of a well-written surprise ending, the answers to the biggest riddles of life clicked in place in a way that seems so obvious in hindsight. How could I not see these truths before!? That I do not know. "One thing I do know. I was blind, but now, I see."[2]

As I acclimated to this new vision of the world, what seemed foolish now seemed obvious. It used to seem rather foolish to me how someone could have such faith in God, yet now it seems obvious that there must be a Creator antecedent to a creation. It used to seem foolish to believe in the Resurrection, and now it seems obvious that the pervasiveness of historical evidence suggesting a human around 2,000 years ago claimed to be God, died, and rose from the dead exists precisely because such an event happened.

---

[1] Saint Augustine and Henry Chadwick, trans, *Confessions* (Oxford: Oxford University Press, 1991), 8.

[2] Jon 9:25. All Bible citations unless noted are from the *New International Version* (2011).

On the flip side, some things previously seemed obvious, but I have now realized they warrant serious reconsideration. One such example is a point raised by C.S. Lewis about the morality of lending at interest. It's better to read Lewis than me, so I'll quote him in full.

"There is one bit of advice given to us by the ancient heathen Greeks, and by the Jews in the Old Testament, and by the great Christian teachers of the Middle Ages, which the modern economic system has completely disobeyed. All these people told us not to lend money at interest; and lending money at interest - what we call investment - is the basis of our whole system. Now it may not absolutely follow that we are wrong. Some people say that when Moses and Aristotle and the Christians agreed in forbidding interest (or 'usury' as they called it), they could not foresee the joint stock company, and were only thinking of the private money lender, and that, therefore we need not bother about what they said. That is a question I cannot decide on. I am not an economist and I simply do not know whether the investment system is responsible for the state we are in or not. This is where we want the Christian economist. But I should not have been honest if I had not told you that three great civilizations had agreed (or so it seems at first sight) in condemning the very thing on which we have based our whole life."[3]

The claim that lending at interest is sinful (which throughout the book I will use interchangeably with the term usury in its historical sense of lending at *any* interest) was rather shocking to me, to say the least. I had never heard this question seriously raised before, and even the most knowledgeable Christians I knew had nary a word on the matter. And yet, as I dug into the question, I found the evidence from scripture and church tradition to appear overwhelmingly in favor of the claim that lending at interest is, in fact, sinful. Further to the point, serious counterarguments were difficult to find, and the most common retorts reeked of "chronological snobbery" by those who would confidently dismiss the question as outdated and silly to even ask.

The evidence suggesting that lending at interest (or usury) is sinful and that we, as the Body of Christ, not to mention basically every nation and major economy in the world today, are blatantly

---

[3] C. S. Lewis, *Mere Christianity* (San Francisco: Harper Collins, 1980), 85.

disobeying God's commands has gnawed at me too much to ignore. Therefore, I am writing to persuade you what I now firmly believe - lending at interest is sinful, we have strayed horribly from God's law on the matter, and we should expect frightening consequences If we don't repent.

Since I am not an economist and don't quite fit the mold of who Lewis suggested should engage this question, I'll be following Chesterton's wisdom when he says - "If a thing is worth doing, it is worth doing badly."[4] I am writing out of nothing but passion on this topic, which certainly makes me an amateur writer in the historical sense of the word. If one considers the amateur label to apply in any other way to this writing, I ask the reader to show me grace and be open to any truth that can be gleaned despite the failings of the messenger.

Ultimately, I see no real option to stay silent on this topic "…if I say, 'I will not mention his word or speak anymore in his name,' his word is in my heart like a fire, a fire shut up in my bones. I am weary of holding it in; indeed, I cannot."[5] As I write, I pray for God to guide my thoughts and correct and forgive me for my errors. I pray for God to reveal His love and truth to anyone reading this, and I plead for God to forgive and have mercy on us if we've truly strayed as far as I fear from His Word.

---

[4] G. K Chesterton, *The Paradoxes of Mr. Pond* (1937).

[5] Jeremiah 20:9.

2. What Is This Thing We Call Money?

"If we offend the principles of reason our religion will be absurd and ridiculous" - Blaise Pascal[6]

Having bent many ears rambling about usury, I've found that interlocutors on this topic typically respond similarly. They respond to a *moral* claim against usury with an *economic* claim favoring it. This pattern seems to play out the same regardless of how the moral claim is grounded. To someone who claims scripture as the ultimate source of authority, you would expect an argument condemning usury through scripture to be countered by continuing to affirm the authority of scripture, except to explain how it has been misinterpreted in this instance to condemn something incorrectly. The same goes for one who claims church tradition as an authority - you would expect a counterargument against the condemnation of usury to continue using these same grounds of tradition, except to explain how it has been misinterpreted or misapplied.

And yet, that is not how these dialogues typically go. A Protestant will respond to Moses or King David with Adam Smith or Friedrich Hayek, and a Catholic will respond to Aquinas or Pope Leo the Great by quoting John Maynard Keynes or Milton Friedman. While I ground my conviction that usury is sinful in scripture, starting with a scriptural argument on this matter would be fruitless - none of us would have ears to hear. We have economic concerns at the top of our minds, and therefore, I believe the argument against usury can best be presented by addressing these concerns first.

For the purposes of clarity, we will bucket the economic objections into micro-level objections, and macro-level objections. The micro-level objections are those considering an individual loan arrangement, whereas the macro-level objections relate to interest's role in the overall economy. Common micro-level economic objections include the following - "Isn't interest just compensating the lender for their risk?" "Shouldn't interest be charged to cover the opportunity cost of lending money?" "Doesn't the time value of money justify interest?" These micro-level objections will be

---

[6] Peter Kreeft, *Christianity for Modern Pagans* (San Francisco: Ignatius Press, 1966), 237.

addressed in detail in a later section, so we will put them to the side for now.

I would, however, like to focus on the common macro-level objections raised in favor of usury. While these macro-level objections will be revealed through questions phrased differently, they are really getting at the same concerns. Someone may be wondering, "Without interest, who would lend me the money to pay for college?" "How could I buy a house or car without a loan?" "How could my business function without credit?" These concerns are quite reasonable - it's becoming increasingly difficult for even the thriftiest among us to fathom living without some form of debt.

If these concerns are extended beyond individual households and businesses, they tap into even deeper existential economic questions - *how could our economy function without lending, and who would lend without the incentive of interest?* This next statement may come as a surprise to the reader, but I will concede the claim that our economy *in its current form* could not function without lending, and without the incentive of interest then there would not be enough lending to sustain the economy.

Conventional wisdom of the day declares that interest is good because the incentive to lend at interest spurs lending, and lending provides the monetary lubrication needed to sustain our economy. In other words, the ultimate end of sustaining the economy justifies the means of usury. However, I find this line of thinking quite puzzling. Why should we so earnestly desire an economy that can only be sustained through perpetual lending? I think we have the situation precisely backward. We think usury is justified because it sustains the economy, but in reality, it is a teetering house of cards largely *because* of usury.

To expand on this claim, we must first understand what we call money. Definitions of money tend to revolve around its role as a medium of exchange, a store of value, and a unit of account. While most definitions are in the same ballpark, finding consensus can be surprisingly challenging. Some emphasize the defining characteristic of money as its role as a medium of exchange; others insist that to be money, it must also be a store of value. Most will point to the dollar bill as the most obvious example of money, while others will demand this not be called money as it's not a true store of value. While I'm wary of adding to the cacophony of voices defining this peculiar thing, there are two aspects of money that I believe to be essential to understanding the points I intend to make throughout this writing that often go unnoticed. The definitions of money typically speak to what it's made of and its purpose. For example, money may be defined as a store of value and unit of account (purpose) and made of coins, paper, or digital currency (material). People may debate the nuances of the material that makes up money and the purpose of money, but the debate usually resides within these spheres. However, you rarely find definitions that speak to money's *efficient* cause - the source of change that creates money, or money's *formal* cause -the essence of the thing itself. Therefore, I will incorporate these components in a definition of money for the purposes of this writing and emphasize these points where they are most germane to the arguments I am making. One need not fully agree with this definition to follow the argument I am trying to make, but for the sake of this writing, I consider money to be anything that is a quantitative representation of value independent of itself, *created and sustained by faith*. I will expound on the essence, or formal cause of money, in a later section, but I would first like to elaborate on the efficient cause of money.

Money's existence depends on faith. Specifically, faith that someone else will accept your money in exchange for goods, services, or as a repayment of debt. This faith can be applied to physical objects such as gold or silver, digital objects such as cryptocurrency, claims to another object (such as a banknote redeemable for gold), claims of credit corresponding to another's debt, or government decrees that demand the use of a certain type of currency. Sometimes, faith in money may spring up voluntarily and cooperatively, and at other times, faith in money may result from a compulsory edict. Even when a state entity compels the use of a certain type of money, that money's existence is still maintained by faith. The belief that others will continue to accept a medium of exchange may be grounded in confidence in the integrity of the state issuing the currency or the power of the state to continue to compel the use of this medium of exchange, but it's ultimately still faith that others will accept this medium of exchange that sustains that money's existence. I have emphasized the role of faith in money because I believe our modern *monetary* faith offends the principles of reason. In an ironic twist, a world forged on the foundations of the Age of Reason spurns reason and relies on a naive form of faith when it comes to money matters.

Part 1: Early Money

To further elaborate on the claim that money depends upon faith, let me first explain our current monetary system and the different monetary systems that have existed in history. For the sake of simplicity, the historical evolutions of money will be painted in rather broad-brush strokes, and the details will focus on the United States and England. However, the concepts explained will be universal and apply to the evolution of most of our current monetary systems. While there are nuances in the perspectives of what exactly constitutes a monetary system and the evolution of one system to the next, prevailing views will hover around something like the following breakdown of monetary systems:

1) Barter[7]
2) Commodity money
3) Receipt or representative money
4) Fractional money
5) Fiat money without central banks
6) Central banks with fractional commodity reserves
7) Purely fiat central banks without commodity reserves

Barter is trading goods or services between multiple parties without using an exchange medium such as money. For example, if I had grain and my neighbor had a cow, I could barter my grain in exchange for my neighbor's cow. This works great if I have what another party wants and vice-versa; however, what if I have grain and want a cow, but my neighbor who has the cow does not want grain? Situations such as these present challenges to a barter system as an exchange will only occur when two parties each hold

---

[7] I'd be remiss not to at least mention that there are compelling arguments from anthropologists suggesting that the first economic systems were a form of communal debt through trusted relations as opposed to barter (see David Graeber's "Debt: the First 5000 Years"). For example, if neighbor A wanted grain from neighbor B, but they did not meet the double coincidence of wants, neighbor B would give the grain to neighbor A, and neighbor A would simply "owe him one". An economy operating on these imprecise means of tracking debt should really not sound that foreign - we do it all the time in small doses today. You may buy lunch for your friend knowing that next time he'll pick up the tab, or you may move your brother-in-law into his new apartment knowing that he would "owe you one" that you could cash in when you had to put together a new playset for your kids. Economies of this type would periodically gather as a whole community and settle debts amongst the community so things would not get too out of whack. In these types of communities, barter would occur between different communities or tribes where there were not established relationships, but they would not use barter within the tribes or communities themselves. Whichever system came first is mostly beside the point I am trying to make, except it does raise interesting questions on how far we have evolved (or strayed) from our ancestors on economic matters.

an item the other wants - a situation known as a double coincidence of wants. The rarity of the double coincidence of wants aligning motivates individuals to trade for items that are popular as they would have a greater likelihood of exchanging a popular item than they would an unpopular item.

Given these incentives, certain goods would be consistently desired over others. The items that have risen to the top of the monetary food chain have varied widely, including obvious examples such as gold and silver to less obvious examples such as cigarettes, seashells, rice, and tobacco. As a particular item became more popular, it would create a virtuous cycle of increasing demand for this item as folks would seek this popular item out as an intermediary step for an exchange that otherwise would not have been possible. For example, if I had extra grain and wanted a cow, and my neighbor had an extra cow but did not want grain, I would need to find something that my neighbor (who had the extra cow) would want to complete the trade. If gold had become more popular in our community, then I may have better luck finding someone who had gold to trade for my grain first, and then subsequently trading my newly acquired gold for my neighbor's extra cow. If this type of cycle repeats enough, then eventually, something such as gold will become valuable not only because of its use value but also because of its exchange value - the *faith* that one could trade this item for something else they desired. This type of money is called commodity money because an item such as a commodity would often be the one to rise to the top of the monetary food chain. Wheat may *initially* be desired as a food source or gold as an ornamental item, while only eventually garnering value relating to their ability to be used in exchange consistently.

While the reasons for their popularity can be debated, it's a rather uncontroversial fact of history that precious metals such as gold or silver consistently became a standard means of exchange. These metals would be traded based on their weight, and thus, corresponding systems to verify the weight of coins during exchanges were also developed. Government "minting" functions were initially created to certify the weight of a gold or silver coin. Of course, there were still opportunities for deceit through coin debasement (e.g., shaving off the gold from a one-ounce coin so that its weight is less than one ounce while still representing the coin to equal one ounce), and it should come as no surprise that individuals and governments would practice this deceptive scheme on occasion.

Despite the imperfections of the precious metal exchange system, trade often flourished under these conditions. However, as the scale and distance of trade increased, so did the risks and inconveniences of carrying large quantities of precious metals for trading. A trader carrying a cargo load full of gold coins presented an inviting target for a robber, especially if the trader traveled large distances between towns.

Reasons such as this generated demand for a safe location to store gold coins, and naturally, human ingenuity stepped up to meet this demand. Goldsmiths already had the means to store their gold safely, so why not offer a safe place to store someone else's gold? On these occasions, goldsmiths would store an individual's gold for safekeeping, and the goldsmiths would present a "receipt" for an individual to retrieve their gold upon demand. As folks gained faith that these "receipts" could be redeemed for gold, these receipts themselves would represent the value of the gold and would often be traded without redeeming the receipt for gold each time. Thus, receipt, or representative money, was birthed. The "receipts" represented a claim to something perceived as valuable, such as gold.

Part 2: Funny Money

Up to the point of receipt currency, I have nothing really negative to say about the evolution of monetary systems. Like all systems, receipt currency and commodity money systems have imperfections that can be highlighted when humans act with ill will towards one another, but monetary faith remains grounded in reason, and flourishing flows from this reasonable faith. The reasoned faith of participants in these systems enables all sorts of division of labor and division of resource benefits that would otherwise be smothered by the rampant suspicions of an exclusively barter system. What a blessing when humans build harmonies with one another so the gifts and resources bestowed upon us can be magnified to the glory of God. If one is rich in grain and the other in iron, let them cooperate so both can be well-fed and industrious. If one loves cultivating nature, let him lead our farming. If another discovers beautiful melodies, let her write our songs. Ahhh, what a wonderful world this could be.

But alas, systemic trust on this earth sways across a tightrope with gusts of greed and deception threatening the precarious balance between order and anarchy. With the growth of receipt currency, the conditions materialized for a new grifting technique to prey on monetary faith - fractional lending. With the growth of receipt currency, integrity alone stood in the way of a goldsmith (basically serving as a banker in this context) representing *more receipts* than what he had in gold reserves. For example, if a goldsmith had 100 ounces of gold in storage, he may choose to lend paper receipts totaling 200 ounces of gold. In this situation, the lending goldsmith would receive *gold* from the borrower upon settlement of these paper loans for the loaned amount plus any interest associated with the loan. This linguistic alchemy of transforming empty promises into gold birthed fractional currency systems.

There's a word we use in nearly every other situation where one deceives for financial gain - fraud. And yet when one lends more than they have, we call it *fractional* lending, not fraud. How brilliant! Why not take this practice on the road and apply it to all walks of life? Historically, we've been so harsh on business owners who inflate earnings to boost their bonuses (and perhaps egos) - but why!? They are just accounting for fractional profit. And the check fraudster we sanctimoniously condemn - he's just writing checks on a fractional balance.

Fractional reserve apologists, of course, have a response to these critiques of fraud. The system is predicated on the idea that only a fraction of individuals will want their money redeemed at a time, and therefore, the goldsmiths only need to hold enough reserves to cover the amount of money that could be expected to be redeemed at the same time. Just as a juggler can maintain three bowling pins in motion, the thinking goes that fractional reserve banking can maintain a velocity of the money supply such that it does not fail. And just as the juggler truly can keep bowling pins in motion for a period, the fractional reserve sleight of hand can show the appearance of success, at least for a little while. However, neither the juggler nor the fractional reserve system can last - the juggler's strength fails, and the fractional lending system crashes under the weight of its deception. There will inevitably be requests to redeem receipt currency greater than the sum of the gold reserves on deposit, which results in a "bank run." With a bank run, the jig is up, and folks realize that there is not enough gold to back their paper money, and the presumed value of the paper money vanishes into the ether as everyone rushes to collect whatever fraction of the gold that really exists.

Despite these challenges, fractional lending practices still reign supreme and, for all intents and purposes, are still prevalent in nearly all large modern banking systems today[8]. Their continued existence mystifies me as fractional lending practices require exceptional faith that offends the principles of reason. Reason would suggest that a system dependent upon continued faith in a deception would not sustain, and empirical evidence of bank runs throughout the last few centuries proves that, in fact, it does not sustain. And yet here we remain with our monetary faith and the existence of money in this type of system tethered to promises that spurn the laws of mathematics.

While we desperately cling to the false promises of fractional lending, blithely ignoring the screams of reason urging us to let go of our naive faith, something must still be done with those pesky bank runs, or the natives will grow restless. These bank runs present us with an inflection point like the famous musings of Kierkegaard in the book *Fear and Trembling* surrounding the biblical account of Abraham's sacrifice of Isaac. Amid Sarah enduring barrenness for years, the Lord had promised Abraham that Sarah would be blessed with a son and "will be the mother of nations; kings of peoples will come from her." And well into their old age, when all hope of the promise being fulfilled would seem lost, the Lord graciously provided Sarah with laughter and a son named Isaac. And then the unthinkable happens - the Lord calls for Abraham to sacrifice Isaac. How could this make sense!? God promised that the covenant would be established with Isaac, and yet now God calls for Isaac to be sacrificed (Gen 17:19)!?

Under all conceivable interpretations of this situation, ethics and reason demand that Abraham spare Isaac; however, faith in this context calls for a suspension of ethics in pursuit of a greater end - a "teleological suspension of the ethical." Abraham's faith in the righteousness that God will bring about in this event transcends

---

[8] I caveat this claim as some will argue modern financial systems are no longer based on fractional reserve lending because banks can essentially lend to anyone who wants a loan without consideration to reserves as the "reserves" that buttress their loans are nothing more than an entry in a computer system by the Federal Reserve without any limits. So the thinking goes that banks are not lending on a fraction of their reserves, because they can get as many reserves as they want. This view holds merits to its precision, but I find it more confusing than helpful in trying to understand the banking system.

anything discernible by reason. This leap on the strength of the absurd embraces an action even when reason suggests an alternative approach.

Such is our situation with bank runs. Reason would suggest that if a bank fails because it misrepresents the availability of the money it has on deposit, we should return to a system that accurately reflects the money that banks have on deposit. If you want banks to stop failing, the answer is quite simple - have them stop lying. Reason and ethics demand that we turn back and reckon with the cold hard truth of our lending lies before things get worse, but the sirens of monetary faith whisper something so seductive in the distance. "Lend more, not less. Just print them money, and all will be blessed."

Do we return to the arms of reasoned faith, or do we spurn reason and leap across the abyss on the strength of the absurd in pursuit of something greater? "The knight of faith is kept awake, for he is under constant trial and can turn back in repentance to the universal at any moment, and this possibility can just as well be a temptation as the truth."[9] Ought we return home to reason, or is reason merely a temptation against our progressive leap towards this monetary "teleological suspension of the ethical"? For better or worse, history offers us many such monetary knights of faith who have taken this leap on the strength of the absurd and claimed to find solid ground in the land of fiat money. But what are we to make of this fiat money? Were we gifted monetary rams in the thicket to save us from the consequences of our fraudulent lending, or have we been deceived into a prison of our own making? Let us examine how these systems work to make a proper discernment.

Fiat money, in its most unadulterated form, is rather easy to comprehend. Fiat means "*let it be done*" in Latin, and that's basically how it operates. First, a government will choose their favorite number; next, they will decide on a picture of a trustworthy and revered statesman; then, they will decide how to reference the most popular deity of the population. Then, they must find an aesthetically pleasing way to fit these three items on a rectangle. After recuperating from the mental exhaustion of the design process, a government official will take the design to a printing mechanism of their choice, configure the design into the system, and press "print."

---

[9] Soren Kierkegaard, *Fear and Trembling* (London: Penguin Classics, 2003),105

Then, a government official with an authoritative name such as "John" will stroll to the podium with a stately gait, crack a soft smile to accentuate his symmetrical face, and lower the timbre of his voice as he declares that the printed paper is now money. John will also enthusiastically detail the government programs that are ready to exchange human labor and natural resources for these sheets of paper. Although somewhat subdued in the messaging, John will intimate the mechanisms to enforce the transubstantiation of the paper to money. Perhaps John will go with "the stick" and compel that the money be accepted under threat of penalty or force, or maybe John will bluff "the carrot" and promise that the fiat money could be redeemed for gold or silver (although one may reasonably wonder why the government would need to print money on paper that could be redeemed for gold or silver if they had that gold or silver on hand). After the speech has concluded and the bluff goes uncalled, the fiat money machine can be put in motion and repeated to print as much money as needed.

Fiat money systems in this unconcealed form are rare now, but they enjoyed brief reigns at times and places in history. Marco Polo observed fiat money systems such as this during his voyages to China in the 13th century, and the American colonies leveraged this type of system to finance the Revolutionary War.[10] It's not difficult to grasp the appeal of these systems from a government's perspective, especially during times of war. It's quite expensive to equip hundreds of thousands of humans with devices to kill other humans, not to mention the costs of logistics and food to support this effort. The funds to procure the resources and labor to accomplish these things must be taxed, borrowed, or printed. Taxing and borrowing make the true cost of the endeavor much more apparent, which threatens the morale of the soldiers and the civilians. But if money can be printed and decreed, governments can spend whatever they want with the true cost being mostly concealed.

Imagine a game of Monopoly where each of the four players are industriously acquiring their properties, only to be interrupted by a fifth player who did not even want to play the game but rather just wanted to acquire money from everyone else to build guns and such. It would be quite a nuisance for that fifth player to repeatedly ask each of the other four players to provide some of their money so

[10] G. Edward Griffin, *The Creature from Jekyll Island: A Second Look at the Federal Reserve* (Westlake Village: American Media, 2010), 155-156.

that this fifth player could buy guns. No one else cares about guns; they want property. But what if instead of asking for or demanding money, the fifth player simply reached his hand into the game box, pulled out several fresh five-hundred-dollar bills, and told player A that he would give him $50,000 in exchange for player A to divert some of his time he planned to spend expanding the Reading Railroad, and would focus on building bullets and bayonets instead. $50,000! Player A only had $1,000 so he would be thrilled and gladly take the opportunity to earn the additional funds. Of course, the fifth player shrewdly failed to mention that he also had deals with Player B, Player C, and Player D to trade each of them $50,000 from the Monopoly box, too.

After the fifth player has the bullets he needs and the other players are flush with cash, they proceed back to the game, except in this game, the prices of the properties are not fixed; they fluctuate with supply and demand. Before the injection of funds from the fifth player, the total money supply was only $4,000, and each property went for around $200. With these original prices in mind, each player could not wait for their chance to buy the entire board! Except when the first property came up for sale, something strange happened. Player A offered $200 for a property and was already Pinteresting designs for a newly remodeled kitchen, only to be outbid by Player B, who offered $1000. $1000!? Player A bemoaned how recently $1000 would have bought an entire town, and now that's the cost of one property! So next time a property goes up for bid, Player A offers $5,000. While he's upset at the price increase, he consoles himself as this is still just a fraction of his net worth. Player A still does not win the property with $5,000 - this time, he's outbid by Player C, who creeps in with an offer of $10,000. Player A stomps around the game board, muttering to himself. "$10,000!? $10,000!? How does a property cost $10,000!?" At that point, it hits him - they've all been duped. Each player is no better off with $51,000 than when they all had $1,000. Their $51,000 today buys them the same amount of property as their $1,000 did before the injection of fiat money to finance the war. Of course, they are at least much better off than the sixth player, Player F, who retired at Baltic Avenue years ago and will now struggle to live off his fixed income of $10 a month, even though just a few years ago, that was more than enough for all his expenses.

Each of these players has just experienced inflation, or a decrease in the purchasing power of their money. Everyone in this situation loses - except, of course, the fifth player. The fifth player was able to create and spend money with impunity and enjoy the purchasing power of spending this money *before* inflation kicked in. However, much to the chagrin of the fifth player or the government producing fiat currency money, the reality of this system inevitably reveals itself. Humans are gullible, but we're not quite that gullible. People catch on to the idea that you can't just print money forever without repercussions. Therefore, this inflation chicanery can only last so long before the natives demand a change.

But what are we to do now? At this stage in our monetary evolution, we've got two problems: fractional reserve lending results in bank runs, and fiat money results in inflation. Of course, we could just demand that banks stop lending more money than they have and public officials stop printing fiat money[11] - but where's the fun in that? If only we could come up with a more complicated solution that did not solve either of these problems but only obscured them in a convoluted mess that hardly anyone could understand. Ask, and you shall receive! Welcome the central banking system to our history of monetary evolution.

Part 3: The Great Charade

Evil masquerades as good, and the greatest evils masquerade as the greatest Good. Whereas the Unitarianesque fiat money system only deceives briefly, the unholy trinity of central banking systems has the endurance to deceive for quite a while. At its core, central banking systems do not do or achieve anything different than other fiat money systems - they fail spectacularly at their stated goal of price stability by inflating away the value of money (just ask your grandfather or uncle how much a bottle of Coke or a gallon of gas cost when they were growing up if you don't believe me); however, central banking systems shroud these failures much more effectively than other fiat money regimes.

---

[11] This is, of course, an oversimplification as inflation can and has happened with commodity money and fully backed reserve systems. If a considerable influx of gold enters an economy with gold as its currency, then prices will rise much the same as a massive influx of fiat money. Two key differences exist, though - something such as gold exists in a finite amount, which limits the amount that can be injected into the economy, and the amount of resources dedicated to gold mining is dictated by the free market. Therefore, if there were a gold rush that led to inflation and a decrease in the purchasing power of gold, people would eventually quit mining for gold, which would lower the input of gold into the system and eventually lead to a stabilization in price.

Central banks started in the 17th century in Europe, with one of the most prominent and successful versions, the Bank of England, being chartered in 1694. Necessity truly is the mother of invention. England needed money for war, but they could not borrow money due to a recent history of government loan defaults. They feared increased taxes could lead to unrest in the populace, so they found a better way to get what they wanted with the Bank of England.[12] While the Bank of England did the same two things other banks at that time did - it printed paper that could supposedly be redeemed for gold, and it made loans at interest - it did so with the public backing of the government. With this beautiful little quid pro quo, the government would attest to the reliability of the bank, and the bank would lend money at interest back to the government. The bank would have its profits, and the government would have its money for war. Sounds like a win-win, right?

It's a win for the Bank of England and the government but a loss for everyone else. When the government owes money plus interest to someone, how do you imagine they receive the funds to pay back their creditor? Taxes, of course. So, the royal subjects are ultimately the ones on the hook to pay back the loans taken out by the government; however, instead of transparently taxing the populace for the full amount needed before purchases are made, the taxes can be spread out over years, even though the interest charges will result in a higher aggregate amount paid in taxes than would have been paid without the loan. But that's just the start - as the central bank creates money through fractional lending and the government spends it into circulation, inflation occurs, thus reducing the purchasing power of the existing money in circulation. To top it all off, as the central bank lends more money than the gold they hold in reserve, it is just adding to the financial system's instability.

It may seem incredible that the public would fall for this ruse, but when one stokes fear and falsely claims that it is the solution to said fear, humans prove to be quite malleable. Britons presumably feared their money was unsafe with banks due to the threat of bank runs, and a bank certified to be secure would quell these fears. Of course, the Bank of England was never any more secure than other banks - it lent on a fraction of its reserves just like everyone else - but who's to say the truth should get in the way of such a compelling myth?

---

[12] Griffin, *The Creature from Jekyll Island*, 175.

And speaking of these other banks, now seems like a good time to explain their role as the final piece of the central banking tripod before we go much further. In a central banking system, the role of commercial banks is much the same as before - they receive deposits and lend money at interest - but there are two main differences in how they perform these functions. The first is a trend towards uniformity and consolidation in the currency issued by banks - instead of several banks each having their currency, the commercial banks begin using the banknotes from the central bank as the new standard. The second is the type of reserves that are held - before central banks, a commercial bank would create receipt currency to be redeemed in specie.[13] They would lend based on their reserves of specie, whereas in central banking systems, the commercial banks will often hold the central bank's currency as its reserve base for fractional lending.

So, with the unholy trinity of central banking systems, you have the deadbeat dad, the central bank, making promises that will never be kept; you have the spoiled child, the government or treasury, wanting the whole world and wanting it now; and you have the unholy ghost, the commercial banks, spreading the misery of this dysfunction throughout the rest of the population. While its flapping wings have frozen the Cocytus for over three centuries in much the same way, there are some nuances in how these frigid financial gales manifest themselves that are worth understanding.

The first iteration of the Bank of England we discussed is a gold standard system with fractional reserve lending backed by commodities, the same as the deregulated and decentralized fractional reserve banking systems, except the confidence-building requirements for specie reserves ultimately lie with the central bank. In contrast, the reserve requirements for commercial banks may be supplemented by central banknotes instead of gold or silver. And yet, whether by dictum or practice, the reserves held by central and commercial banks are not close to the only amount that would keep them truly sustainable - 100%. Therefore, both central and commercial banks cannot meet their obligations. With commercial banks, "runs" occur where more depositors want their reserves back

---

[13] For the sake of simplicity, I will use gold, silver, and specie interchangeably over the next few pages. In reality, the metal backing of banks and central banks oscillated back and forth from gold to silver, while at times allowing redemption of both, but the type of commodity backing at hand is mostly beside the points I am trying to make, so we will leave these details alone for now.

either in the form of specie or central bank notes than the commercial banks can provide, and with the central bank, more depositors want gold or silver than can be provided. These financial institutions lend more than they have and yet promise that all deposits could still be redeemed for their specie backing if desired. These promises are still nothing more than a confidence game solely dependent on whether enough people want to redeem their money simultaneously.

Reason would, of course, suggest to just stop lending on fraction to end the bank runs. Instead, we come up with solutions drifting us further into absurdity, such as the lender of last resort principle that claims to solve our commercial bank run problems. As the lender of last resort, the central bank provides the reserves needed to satisfy depositor demands to quell the threat of a commercial bank run. While this may sound especially chivalrous, remember that by this stage in the financial evolution, commercial banks no longer require gold reserves; they just require central bank notes, so all the central bank does in this situation is print money. I certainly don't mean to disparage the fine folks at Kinko's with this next statement, but I would hope an army of PhDs could come up with something better than a solution we could get from any printing company. Of course, this paper printing does not solve the problems of financial instability; it just temporarily satiates demand while exacerbating the underlying reality of the already tenuous position of a central bank to be able to redeem its banknotes.

So eventually enough depositors come for the central bank and demand to redeem their banknotes for specie, and we once again have the threat of a bank run and a loss of confidence in the financial system - this time with the central bank itself. Of course, we could admit the whole thing is a sham so we can finally start the actual work to restore our tattered economies, but instead, we invent new ways to kick the can down the road by ceasing the redemption of gold by the central bank. And yes, this is as simple as it sounds - the central bank just says, "So I know I said you could have gold back for this paper I gave you, but it turns out you can't. Sorry. Oh yeah, but don't forget to pay your interest on the loans you took with us. Those are definitely still due". The tragically comical part of all of this is how quickly the absurdity reveals itself - the Bank of England could not even make it two full years without Parliament allowing the Bank of England to renege on its promises to convert bank notes into specie.[14] Now, to their credit, I must admit that while central banks often ceased the convertibility of paper notes for gold, especially during times of war, they sometimes restored to a specie-backed standard after things had settled. At least for a little while, until these promises inevitably became impossible to maintain.

As an oversimplification, we could summarize monetary history from the late 17th century to the early 20th century with a famous quote from Hegel - "But what experience and history teach is this — that peoples and governments never have learned anything from history."[15] Much of the world in the 18th, 19th, and early 20th centuries oscillated between variations of the systems described thus far, with the results playing out rather predictably. Fractional banks failed, fiat money systems inflated, and greed and fear were likely at the root of many of our decisions. In the US, the Bank of the United States, a central bank, was chartered in 1791. It barely missed out on renewing its 20-year charter in 1811 after fierce political battles, thus returning to fractional banking without a central bank. In 1816, a 20-year charter was given to the Second Bank of the United States. After fierce political battles, it narrowly missed out on renewing its 20-year charter in 1836, thus returning to fractional banking without a central bank. In the 1860s, as often happens during times of war, the United States returned to good old-fashioned pure fiat money in the form of "greenbacks," leading to rampant inflation and a mess to clean up after the war.[16]

Ultimately, though, the United States eventually landed in the same situation as England with a central banking system. Although the United States flirted with the idea for centuries, she did not wed herself in unholy matrimony to a central banking system until the early 20th century, when the Federal Reserve Act of 1913 was passed. The origin and the evolution of the Federal Reserve operated much like the original Bank of England charter, beginning with claims of a gold-backed currency while eventually drifting into pure fiat money without any commodity backing.

Now before we dive into our current purely fiat central banking system, where there is no longer even any fractional commodity backing, I think we would benefit from reflecting on two major

---

[14] Griffin, *The Creature from Jekyll Island*, 179.

[15] Georg Wilhelm Friedrich Hegel, *The Philosophy of History* (Ontario: Batoche Books, 2001).

[16] Griffin, *The Creature from Jekyll Island*, 325-395.

themes that have revealed themselves throughout the evolution of money - an increase in the centralization of power and a decrease in the reasonableness of our faith in money as these monetary systems have "progressed" from commodity money to receipt currency, to fractional lending, to fractional central banking, and ultimately to purely fiat central banking systems.

With commodity money (and fully backed receipt currency where the commodity still serves as the source), the power to introduce new money into the system is distributed and available to anyone who can physically obtain the commodity used as money. With *distributed* fractional reserve banking systems (before central banks), any bank could introduce new money into the system with their issuance of receipt currency, and any individual or group that could physically obtain the commodity used as backing could also introduce new money into the system.

With central banks (still backed by commodities), things take a decisive turn towards centralized power, with the central banks controlling how much money the distributed banks could create. However, anyone who acquired a commodity used for backing could still introduce new money into the system. Eventually, with pure fiat money central banking systems, the central bank almost entirely controls the decisions determining money creation. While the decentralized banks can still lend to create money, they do so based on the rules set forth by the central bank, and the general public is now entirely impotent to contribute to any monetary creation except through acting as a debtor to a creditor such as a bank that lends to create money. So, in broad terms, the power to create money has been trickling down a consolidating funnel such that fewer and fewer institutions and individuals determine the creation of money.

To make the consolidation of power matters even more ominous, not only do these same themes take place *within* a particular nation-state, but they also occur in how the different nation-states relate to one another globally. One area of particular interest supporting this theme is the transition from a *gold standard* to a *gold-exchange standard* international monetary system. The gold standard system has already been discussed - this is where a central bank stands ready to convert its currency into gold upon demand. A central bank would set a rate of exchange for each currency it issued and claim it would exchange one unit of currency for an equivalent amount of gold. For example, the Federal Reserve may issue one dollar and claim it could be redeemed for 1/16 of an ounce of gold. The same would go for the Bank of England and other central banking systems. So, in this type of system, individuals' confidence that a central bank could truly redeem their currency for gold would increase demand for that currency. If I had trusted that England had more gold reserves than other countries, I would have preferred that currency for trade. If I lost trust that a currency could be redeemed for gold, I might be more inclined to cash in the currency of these types for the gold before it was all gone. You can probably already guess the results - nations never actually held 100% of gold reserves for their currencies; they lent on fractional reserves, creating risks of bank runs at the central bank level in this type of system. The next steps on a global scale are almost the same as what happens within a particular nation - just with different names and parties playing the redeemer roles. So, *within* a particular nation, you have individual banks that lend on fraction, and as these fail, a central bank comes in and stands ready to be the confidence-building bank that *really* promises to hold sufficient gold reserves, and therefore, the individual banks no longer hold gold specie, they just promise to be able to redeem in the central bank reserves, and you could go to the central bank with these central bank notes to get your actual gold. With the international system, you have individual nations and their central banking systems that lend on fraction, and as those banks fail, people flock to the most reliable central banking system that promises to be able to redeem its currency for gold. The central banks of the other nations no longer promise to hold gold reserves themselves, rather they will just hold reserves of the central bank that promises to keep your gold safe. And with this, you have the birth of the *gold-exchange* standard of international trade.

This gold exchange standard existed in the 1920s and 1930s. It was rather famously codified at the Bretton Woods Conference in 1944 when the United States and the Federal Reserve System were essentially anointed as the central bank of central banks, and the US dollar was dubbed as the currency of currencies. At Bretton Woods, it was agreed that the US would fix its currency to gold and other countries would fix their currencies to the US dollar. So, presumably, anyone could go to their central bank and exchange that nation's currency for US dollars and then redeem their US dollars for gold at the Federal Reserve. Ultimately, everything would be tied to the US dollar, and the Federal Reserve System really,

really promised to keep the gold safe.[17]

Two new institutions were also created at Bretton Woods to support this agreement - the International Monetary Fund (IMF) and the World Bank. The IMF is an international financial organization that receives funding from nations worldwide and promises to monitor and help maintain the international foreign exchange system and to provide financial assistance to other nations in times of need. The World Bank is an international financial institution that provides loans and grants to the governments of low- and middle-income countries to pursue capital projects. The World Bank has little to do with the main points I'm trying to make, and much has been written by authors more qualified than me on both controversial institutions, so I will keep my points brief here. Whatever one thinks of the IMF, it and the entire Bretton Woods Agreement quite obviously failed in their stated goal to have a sort of gold-exchange standard where the US dollar would be convertible to gold and other currencies would be convertible to the US dollar, as the same thing happened as it always does. The institution that promised to keep its redeemability promises, The Federal Reserve System, in this instance, lent so much more than the gold it had in store, so it could never actually redeem all of its notes for gold. It was just a matter of time before the mirage was revealed.

And on August 15th, 1971, the mirage was revealed when an American president was instructed to "take your son, your only son, whom you love, Reason, and sacrifice Reason as a burnt offering at a location I will show you." "When he reached the place of instruction, he built an altar there and arranged the wood on it, and bound his son, Reason, and laid him on the altar on top of the wood. He then reached out his hand and took the knife to slay his son, Reason." And as Richard Nixon famously signed the executive order that suspended the redemption of US dollars for gold, the last vestiges of any sort of reason undergirding our financial faith were vanquished, and we entered into purely fiat central banking.

Part 4: The Bubble of Bubbles

We have finally arrived at the point where it would be beneficial to explain how money works today in our completely fiat money central

---

[17] *Federal Reserve History*, "Creation of the Bretton Woods System," https://www.federalreservehistory.org/essays/bretton-woods-created

banking system. People are often overwhelmed by how money works and are led to believe this is because it is some complicated, esoteric thing that only financial geniuses can understand. In one sense, that is true - modern money can be exceptionally difficult to comprehend - but the difficulty in comprehension lies not in money's genius but in its stupidity. Modern money is complicated, but it's also quite dumb, and the fact that it's so dumb makes it most difficult to understand. Some stories are difficult to follow because they have such beautiful storylines with interwoven parts that fit together perfectly, and their beauty is revealed in depth the more you think through and study them. In contrast, some stories are difficult to follow simply because they have no point and are full of plot gaps. A seventh grader's term paper may be as difficult to understand as St. Augustine's but for entirely different reasons. If one studies long enough, one may be able to understand how a rocket can propel itself into space, although this rocket science is undoubtedly difficult. However, no matter how long one studies the topic, one will simply be unable to make sense of a worldview that believes "something can come from nothing." Such is the case with modern money - at its core, it demands that we suspend reason and believe absurdities such that "something can come from nothing."

Although money today no longer has any sort of commodity backing, I find it easiest to understand how the system works by comparing it to these previous systems, so we will start with a refresher of what's been covered so far. In a *commodity money* system, something such as gold becomes desired more than other objects not only for its intrinsic use but also for its likelihood to be accepted in trade by others, and thus, it becomes money. In a *receipt currency system*, something like gold will be deposited for safekeeping in banks, and banks will lend "receipts" that are a claim to the gold that they keep secure. In a *fractional reserve system*, banks will lend out more than they have on hand, so if they have 100 ounces of gold, they will lend receipts equaling claims to the redemption of 1000 ounces of gold. In this situation, the banks would call the 100 ounces of gold on deposit a "reserve" that enables them to lend beyond the amount of the 100 ounces of gold initially deposited. In a *central banking fractional reserve system,* the central bank holds the gold and issues central banking notes, or reserves, to the other banks, and the other banks lend to customers based on their reserves of central bank notes. For example, the central bank may have 100 ounces of gold, providing central bank reserves to banks equal to the redemption of 1000 ounces of gold.

Then, the other banks will lend to customers for amounts equal to the redemption of 10,000 ounces of gold based on those central bank reserves that were provided to the bank.

Now in today's *fiat money central banking system,* there is no longer any gold backing the creation of money, so it's easiest to understand money as simply being debt because that's basically what it is now. If one person or institution has money today, it's only because another person or institution has debt. The $100 in my bank account is an asset for me but a liability or a debt for the bank. The bank owes me $100. My mortgage, however, is the exact opposite - it is a liability, or a debt for me, but an asset for the bank. I owe the bank a lot more than $100. A dollar bill now is the same - a credit that can be used to pay for a debt. A dollar used to say, "redeemable in gold on demand at the United States Treasury, or in gold or lawful money at any Federal Reserve Bank," and now it says, "this note is legal tender for all debts, public and private." Your dollar is nothing more than a credit partitioned off from its originating debt.

The fact that money is nothing more than debt can be a confusing paradigm shift when trying to understand the current monetary system, and it becomes even more confusing when trying to understand who owes what to whom and how the money is made in the first place. Our financial deity is three in one - deadbeat dad (central bank), spoiled child (government treasury), and unholy ghost (commercial banks), and all the members of the unholy trinity interact with each other in rather obscure ways. The commercial banks create money by lending to the general public, yet they cannot mint money or create reserves. The central banks seemingly create assets out of thin air through reserves, but they are not the ones who physically print money on a sheet of paper, nor are they the ones who distribute money to us commoners. And the treasury can loan money, spend money, and *mint* or physically print money, but it cannot truly create money. Confused yet? Let's walk through a few common examples explaining how the different members of the unholy trinity operate, hoping that it will help clear things up.

One of the most common and easily understandable methods of monetary creation comes from commercial banks. Let's say a customer buys a fully financed house with a 30-year mortgage from a commercial bank for $500K. In this transaction, the bank loans the customer $500K, the customer pays the home builder $500K, and the home builder deposits $500K back into the bank. The net results for each party are as follows:

- The customer now has an asset (home) valued at $500K and a corresponding liability (mortgage) of $500K.
- The bank has an asset (loan) valued at $500K and a corresponding liability (home builder deposit) of $500K
- The home builder has an asset (bank deposit) valued at $500K and equity of $500K in sales revenue.

In this situation, the bank created $500K when the bank made the loan to the customer to purchase the home, and this should be evident as the home builder, who now has $500K in his checking account, can go and spend that money at other places. If you think it seems a little unfair that the bank can make up dollars out of thin air, it gets much worse, as we're missing one key point - the interest on the loan that the customer owes the bank! Let's assume a 30-year mortgage at around a 5.3% interest rate, such that the total amount due over the loan is $1M.

Assuming the customer earns $1M over the loan's lifetime and pays off the loan in its entirety over the loan duration, the following would occur.

- The customer would still have an asset (home) valued at $500K, and his liability (mortgage) would be paid off so he would now have $500K in equity.
- The bank would now have an asset (cash) valued at $1M, a corresponding liability (home builder deposit) of $500K, and equity of $500K in interest revenue.
- The home builder has an asset (bank deposit) valued at $500K and equity of $500K in sales revenue.

So, the bank does not do anything other than type a few numbers into a spreadsheet, and yet they reap the rewards of 30 years of labor from their loan customer for the same amount of revenue as the builder who built the house. But something else in this situation is even more confusing and troubling. The loan created $500K that was added to the money supply, yet $1M was due to the bank. Where does the remaining $500K come from to pay off the loan!? The total balance of money owed in this economy is $1M, yet the total amount of existing money is only $500K. Well, you may think that's no biggie; the borrower just needs to earn $500K from some other source to pay back the difference. But from where? Whenever a loan is made that creates money with the expectation that interest is paid on the loan, the expectation of money to be received is greater than the money that is being added to the system. Since all new money added to our debt-based system comes through a loan arrangement (which almost always includes the expectation of interest), then the aggregate money owed is greater than the amount that exists in circulation.

That leaves only two options for how the interest could be repaid. The first option is for the borrower to exchange labor or resources in exchange for a repayment of the debt. Imagine an economy with only one borrower and one lender where the lender loans $100 to the borrower, but expects $110 back after interest. The borrower could pay back $100, and then provide his labor to the lender in exchange for the remaining $10 of debt. In this simple example you have an overt fulfillment of Proverbs 22:7 where "the rich rule over the poor, and the borrower is slave to the lender." Ultimately this enslavement occurs either way, but there is a second option that makes the enslavement worse, but defers the consequences by creating more money to pay off the loan by taking on more debt. Since this debt will also require the repayment of interest, then this burden will only become greater as the collective amount of money owed will become increasingly greater than the money that exists.

Therefore, it should come as no surprise that borrowers often default on their mortgages as the burden becomes too great to sustain, which also ends up quite favorably for the bankers. Using the same example from above, let's say a customer buys a fully financed house with a 30-year mortgage from a commercial bank for $500K. In this transaction, the bank loans the customer $500K, the customer pays the home builder $500K, and the home builder deposits $500K back into the bank. Except in this situation, let's assume the customer never makes a payment on the home, and the home is foreclosed by the bank, such that they forcibly take possession of the home. The net results for each party are as follows:

- The customer originally had an asset (home) valued at $500K and a corresponding liability (mortgage) of $500K; however, upon the foreclosure, his asset (home) of $500K and his liability of $500K were both wiped out from his balance sheet, netting to zero.

- The bank originally had an asset (loan) valued at $500K and a corresponding liability (home builder deposit) of $500K; however, upon the foreclosure, the bank now has an asset (home) valued at $500K, a liability (home builder deposit) of $500K, and no longer has a loan asset.
- The home builder has an asset (bank deposit) valued at $500K and equity of $500K in sales revenue.

There's one component that's especially important to notice here - remember, when the bank loaned money to the customer, this was money seemingly made up out of thin air - it did not exist. And yet, when the customer does not repay the loan to the bank, the bank ends up with a house. So, when the bank makes the loan, they conjure up $500K that they never actually had, and in exchange, they either receive $1M ($500K in revenue) or a house. It's a game of "heads, I win" and "tails, you lose."

But wait, it gets even worse. The only thing that could go wrong in this situation for the bank is if it goes insolvent - if they cannot pay back their debts. And remember, the debts for a bank (their liabilities) are primarily customer deposits - the aggregate sum of the accounts for all their customers. So, if customers ask for more money than the bank can pay back, the bank would be insolvent. Of course, the banks can never actually redeem a critical mass of their customers' checking accounts - putting aside the fact that there is nothing even really to redeem, it's all just debt now - the banks do not hold an amount of cash or liquid assets equivalent to their customer deposits. So, it's just a matter of time until the situation occurs where customers want back more from their deposit accounts than the bank can provide. And yet, when this situation occurs, the banks still win. Sure, some banks will be left to fail seemingly at random, but most will not. If too many banks failed, the system would literally implode - money is nothing but debt, and it's nothing but debt tied up in layers upon layers of debt, so if it became apparent that enough banks were unable to meet their debt obligations, the whole thing would collapse quite quickly. Of course, there is a high likelihood this will eventually happen - exponential growth cannot continue in perpetuity, but worries of posterity are far from the minds of the politicians or central bankers at the helm in a crisis - they simply do not want to be the ones to let the whole thing collapse on their watch. So, bank bailouts consistently and inevitably occur. With a bank bailout, the government will either lend money to the banks in distress or perhaps purchase some ownership in the distressed banks until public confidence is restored. And so, from the bank's perspective, their problems are solved - they can keep on lending and receiving their interest revenue or trading made-up money for real assets.

But what about this money that the government pays in these situations? Where does the money come from when it's not generated by the commercial banks? This seems to offer a good segue to explain some other types of monetary generation in our pure fiat money central banking system. Let's take a simple example, such as the issuance of a physical $100 bill, to get a sense of how this works.

In this situation, the Treasury will issue a treasury bill, essentially a promise that the Treasury will pay back a certain amount in the future. So, if someone purchases a $100 Treasury bill, the Treasury may promise to pay back $101 a year from now. Treasury bills can be purchased by many entities - individual investors, corporations, banks, central banks, etc. - but in this situation, we'll assume they are purchased by the Federal Reserve directly to make the example simpler.

So, when the Federal Reserve purchases the treasury bill, it creates a $100 reserve, seemingly from nothing. Then the Federal Reserve swaps the $100 reserve with the Treasury for their $100 treasury security. The following would take place from an accounting perspective:

- Federal Reserve
  - Asset: $100 Treasury Security
  - Liability: $100 Reserves
- Treasury
  - Asset: $100 Reserves
  - Liability: $100 Treasury Security (national debt)

So, all that happens here is the Federal Reserve goes into a computer spreadsheet somewhere and types in the number $100 as a reserve asset. Someone at the Fed will then arrange with someone at the Treasury that they would like to exchange their $100 reserves asset for a treasury bill. After the exchange, the Federal Reserve now has a treasury security as an asset (a promise that the Treasury will pay them back a specified amount of money in the future), and the Treasury now has the "reserves" from the

Federal Reserve as their $100 asset. Once the treasury has $100 in reserves, it can then use these reserves to print a $100 bill physically or spend it however it so chooses.

So, revisiting the statement from earlier, hopefully, you can now see how the commercial banks create money by lending to the general public, the central banks create reserves, and the treasury loans money, spends money, and *mints* or physically prints money.

There is one last key point, though, before we move on. The transaction above simplifies the role of the Federal Reserve in generating reserves for clarity, but it obscures one important factor that happens when treasury securities are purchased with the expectation of interest to be received, which almost always happens. Let's assume a commercial bank purchases a $100 treasury security at 1% annual interest, whereas the Treasury owes the bank $101 at the end of the year. $100 is created with the expectation to receive $101. But where does the other dollar come from for the Treasury to repay this debt? Remember, money is nothing but debt, so this dollar must either be loaned into existence, which would carry the expectation of additional interest that could only be paid if more loans were made to create money, or labor and resources must be exchanged to pay off the debt.

Do you see the unsustainability and absurdity of the system? We either continue the ever-ballooning system of debt by creating new debt to pay off our current debts, or we succumb to the stark reality that the few parties in the world that have the power to generate money through loan agreements have essentially enslaved the entire world by these actions. Money is created through the banking system transferring reserves for treasury securities, and a treasury security is nothing more than a promise that the government will pay back more money than was loaned at some date in the future. This interest must either be paid back through the labor and resources of the taxpayers, or by the government creating additional money (which just balloons the debt obligations). Practically speaking, both of these things typically happen with the resources and labor of the taxpayers paying for the interest on these loans all the while the treasury creates additional loans that expand the overall debt owed.

You will probably hear explanations of this process as something akin to a monetary creation "ex nihilo." The Federal Reserve will be credited with creating these reserve assets out of thin air, but that's not how it works. Something cannot come from nothing. Something physical can come from something spiritual (a la the universe from God), but something cannot come from nothing. This monetary creation "ex nihilo" is not something from nothing; it is transforming something spiritual (our faith) into the propulsive monetary systems that run our entire world.

God is love. The Father, Son, and the Holy Spirit each love the other in a divine dance of sorts, and out of that outpouring of love at the core of the universe springs forth all of creation. At the core of a true, godly economy, gifts would be the core of our system - an outpouring of love towards the other that prompts reciprocation, not to sever a relationship or extinguish a debt, but rather to deepen relationships, trust, and a flowing economy. If you invite someone over for a meal, the natural response is for that person to want to do something kind in return, prompting more kindness from the first person. The beautiful, virtuous cycle sustains and builds friendships - each friend has a natural and godly desire to continue to do good for the other.[18]

And yet how perversely the unholy trinity inverts this dance of other-centered, productive love into a self-centered parasitic orgy of destructive consumption! Our governments create debt obligations on our behalf (as we're the taxpayers who ultimately pay for these things), and our banks put us directly into bondage with debts, knowing full well that these debts will likely never be repaid. And yet, our entire lives are based on these systems that have placed us in complete and perpetual bondage where the likelihood of repayment becomes infinitesimally smaller by the day. It's been said, "The greatest trick the Devil ever pulled was convincing the world he didn't exist." Perhaps a close second is creating a financial system that requires increasing deposits of faith to keep the system afloat even though the system itself, the object of our faith, becomes increasingly absurd with each passing day. I can hardly imagine a more pristinely manicured and ubiquitous path to hell.

Part 5: Castles Made of Sand

Earlier in the book, I claimed that the economy is a teetering house of cards in large part *because* of usury, and I hope the reasons for

---

[18] Marc Barnes and Jacob Iman, hosts. "Redemption." *Good Money,* 21 April 2021, https://newpolity.com/podcasts-hub/redemption

the scenic detour to explain the evolution of money to make this point are now clear. Usury, or lending money at interest, has propelled our financial system into increasing levels of absurdity over the last five centuries as the drive to lend at interest undoubtedly hastened the shift from receipt currency to fractional lending, and from fractional lending to a purely debt-based fiat money central banking system. With each step in the process, we drift from reason to absurdity and from the real to the unreal, and the effects on our souls and world are devastating. A quote from David Hawkes regarding the prevailing views on usury in Renaissance England proves frighteningly prescient for what has come to pass. "Legalized usury commits the human race to the unceasing pursuit of economic growth. Usury imposes an unstoppable expansion on the process of wealth creation; it sets in motion a driving force whose velocity increases exponentially along with compound interest, impelling us to transform all the world's human and natural resources into the form of financial representation. As the people of Renaissance England clearly saw and often said, usury is inherently insatiable. The history of the human race since restraints on usury began to be lifted has involved the sudden and dramatic colonization of the globe by money, the evaluation of human activity and the natural environment in terms of money, and the direction of an ever-increasing proportion of physical and psychological energy towards the production of money."[19]

How are we so foolish! The intellectual hubris of the day leads many to mock any reference to the supernatural. Yet, our faith in money presumes supernatural abilities in this legal fiction, such as the ability to create "something from nothing" or for demands for perpetual exponential growth to coexist with the world's finite resources. I could hardly fathom a more textbook example of idolatry. This entire system screams for a comparison to the story of Daniel and the Babylonian idol Bel. I will quote this story in full as it is probably unfamiliar to many as it comes from chapters no longer in most Protestant Bibles.[20]

"And so Daniel was living with the king, and he was honored above all his friends. Now there was an idol with the Babylonians named

---

[19] David Hawkes, *The Culture of Usury in Renaissance England* (London: Palgrave Macmillian, 2010), 2-3.
[20] Thank you again to Jacob Iman and Marc Barnes of the NewPolity Podcast, *Good Money*, for pointing out how timely this Biblical example is to our day and age.

Bel. And each day there was expended on him twelve great measures of fine flour, and forty sheep, and six vessels of wine. The king likewise worshipped him and went each day to adore him, but Daniel adored his God. And the king said to him, "Why do you not adore Bel?" And answering, he said to him, "Because I do not worship idols made with hands, but the living God, who created heaven and earth, and who holds power over all flesh." And the king said to him, "Does not Bel seem to you to be a living god? Do you not see how much he eats and drinks every day?" Then Daniel said, smiling, "O king, do not make a mistake, for this one is clay on the inside and brass on the outside, and he has never eaten." And the king, being angry, called for his priests and said to them, "If you do not tell me who it is that has eaten these expenses, you will die. But if you can show that Bel has eaten these, Daniel will die, because he has blasphemed against Bel." And Daniel said to the king, "Let it be according to your word." Now the priests of Bel were seventy, besides their wives, and little ones, and sons. And the king went with Daniel into the temple of Bel. And the priests of Bel said, "Behold, we are going out, and you, O king, set out the meats, and mix the wine, and close the door, and seal it with your ring. And when you have entered in the morning, if you have not found that Bel has consumed all, we will suffer death, or else Daniel will, who has lied against us." But they had no concern because they had made a secret entrance under the table, and they always went in through it and devoured those things. And so it happened, after they had departed, that the king set the foods before Bel, and Daniel commanded his servants, and they brought ashes, and he sifted them throughout the temple in the sight of the king, and, as they left, they shut the door, and after sealing it with the king's ring, they departed. But the priests entered by night, according to their custom, with their wives, and their sons, and they ate and drank everything. But the king arose at first light, and Daniel with him. And the king said, "Are the seals unbroken, Daniel?" And he answered, "They are unbroken, O king." And as soon as he had opened the door, the king stared at the table, and cried out with a loud voice, "Great are you, O Bel, and there is not any deceit with you." And Daniel laughed, and he held back the king, so that he would not enter, and he said, "Look at the pavement, notice whose footsteps these are." And the king said, "I see the footsteps of men, and women, and children." And the king was angry. Then he apprehended the priests, and their wives, and their sons, and they showed him the secret doors through which they entered and consumed the things that were on the table. Therefore, the king slaughtered them and delivered Bel into the power of Daniel, who overturned him and his temple" (Daniel 14:1-21).[21]

Such is our situation today. We provide a bounty of sacrifices to the god of money in the form of our time, our labor, our resources, our minds, and just about anything else one could imagine, and we piously lay our sacrifices at the altar of our god - money, the economy, "the market," or whatever other affectionate pet names we have given our lord. And every night, the modern-day priests of Bel, the leaders of the commercial banks, the central banks, and the government treasuries, sneak in through the back door of the Temple of Mammon and consume all the sacrifices we've given him. They do this in monetary creation that only benefits the priestly class of Mammon while weakening the purchasing power of all other money that exists within the laity. They do this by charging interest on money created by the act of the loan itself. And yet, we're too blind to see these things - our devotion is too great to our lord, Mammon, to bother to wonder where all our sacrifices are going.

At this point, I suspect that some who understand these dreadful injustices ingrained in our economic system will eagerly anticipate discussing how we can fix this broken system. I will warn you from the outset that I will offer little valuable information on systemic economic reform in this writing. It's not that I do not want to see the system improved - I desperately do - but I think the roots of our problems are deeper and more fundamental. Any economy only works because the members within that economy have some means to trust one another, whether through relationships, reputations, some intermediary trusted broker, or, in our case, money. Unfortunately, as it exists today, money is untrustworthy - it's nothing but a big lie waiting to be revealed. When the day comes that humans lose our trust in money, basically every interaction as we know it today could be rendered impossible, whether that be purchasing coffee at our local bakery, buying groceries, or paying our mortgage. This scenario is quite frightening, and borders on anarchic.

However, from an optimistic perspective, it's not as if money does anything itself - we cannot eat money, drink money, or use it as a raw material to build a house or a car. Money simply facilitates trust between individuals, and individuals cultivate the land to produce

---

[21] Catholic Public Domain Version.

crops and transform raw resources into usable tools and shelters. So, all we need is a new and better way to trust one another. Sounds easy, right? Of course, that is easier said than done to build trust in a fallen world where "the heart is deceitful above all things and beyond cure."[22] We lack trust because we are untrustworthy.

Hence, we must go back to the fundamentals. I believe usury is a sin, and sin separates and erodes trust. Our entire economic system is built on the sin of usury, and therefore, we must first re-learn the fundamental truth of the sin of usury before we can have any hope of serious and sustainable economic reform. Sometimes, "the longest way round is the shortest way home."[23]

---

[22] Jeremiah 17:9.
[23] Lewis, *Mere Christianity*, 87.

3. For the Bible Tells Me So

"When the king heard the words of the Book of the Law, he tore his robes…'Great is the Lord's anger that burns against us because those who have gone before us have not obeyed the words of this book; they have not acted in accordance with all that is written there concerning us'" (2 Kings 22:11,13).

With the dreadful state of our current economic condition now top of mind, I think we are better prepared to hear what scripture says about usury with "ears to hear and eyes to see." While I am not a professional in this area, thankfully, the interpretation in this situation is rather straightforward - scripture says consistently and unequivocally that lending at interest, or usury, is a sin. In my opinion it requires only a basic level of reading comprehension to see this truth from scripture. It seems to take some form of doctorate to perform the mental contortions necessary to claim both that scripture is authoritative, and usury is *not* sinful.

To correctly understand the proper interpretation of the morality of lending at interest based upon the Bible, I would suggest we first remind ourselves of some obvious themes from scripture relating to money, idolatry, and love. Then assess the rather clear verses on usury to let them inform the unclear ones. And finally, tackle some of the verses relating to usury that appear tricky at first glance and are commonly used to justify why usury was never or is no longer a sin.

Firstly, while I think we can cover these quickly as they are rather uncontroversial and commonly known, we must bear in mind some of the most common and frequent instructions God provides in the Bible relating to the love of money, idolatry, and loving others before approaching something such as usury. These broad and typically universally accepted themes from scripture all jibe neatly with a view that lending at interest is a sin as this act displays an excessive love of money and greed (ignoring what God commands not to do) and refuses opportunities to love the other person in need of a loan (ignoring what God commands to do).

For just a sampling to keep in mind relating to money:

- In Ecclesiastes 5:10, we are warned that "Whoever loves money never has enough; whoever loves wealth is never satisfied with their income."

- In 1 Timothy 6:10, Paul famously writes, "For the love of money is a root of all kinds of evils. It is through this craving that some have wandered away from the faith and pierced themselves with many pangs."
- Jesus himself famously says in Mark 6.24: "No one can serve two masters; for either he will hate the one and love the other, or he will be devoted to one and despise the other. You cannot serve God and wealth."
- Jesus says in Matthew 19:24: "Again I tell you, it is easier for a camel to go through the eye of a needle than for a rich person to enter the kingdom of God."

As it relates to idolatry, remind yourself of the following warnings that are scattered throughout scripture:

- Leviticus 19:4: "Do not turn to idols or make metal gods for yourselves. I am the Lord your God."
- Isaiah 44:9-11: "All who make idols are nothing, and the things they treasure are worthless. Those who would speak up for them are blind; they are ignorant, to their own shame. Who shapes a god and casts an idol, which can profit nothing? People who do that will be put to shame; such craftsmen are only human beings. Let them all come together and take their stand; they will be brought down to terror and shame."
- 1 Corinthians 10:14: "Therefore, my dear friends, flee from idolatry."
- Revelation 9:20: "The rest of mankind who were not killed by these plagues still did not repent of the work of their hands; they did not stop worshiping demons, and idols of gold, silver, bronze, stone and wood—idols that cannot see or hear or walk."
- And in Colossians 3:5, Paul tells us even more explicitly that our greed is idolatry: "Put to death, therefore, whatever belongs to your earthly nature: sexual immorality, impurity, lust, evil desires and greed, *which is idolatry.*"

As it relates to love, remind yourself of just a few examples of these instructions throughout scripture:

- 1 John 3-16:17: "This is how we know what love is: Jesus Christ laid down his life for us. And we ought to lay down our lives for our brothers and sisters. If anyone has material possessions and sees a brother or sister in need but has no pity on them, how can the love of God be in that person?"

- John 15:13: "Greater love has no one than this: to lay down one's life for one's friends."
- Colossians 3:14: "And over all these virtues put on love, which binds them all together in perfect unity."
- 1 Corinthians 13:4-7: "Love is patient, love is kind. It does not envy, it does not boast, it is not proud. It does not dishonor others, it is not self-seeking, it is not easily angered, it keeps no record of wrongs. Love does not delight in evil but rejoices with the truth. It always protects, always trusts, always hopes, always perseveres."

Heed these warnings against greed and idolatry and these commands to love as we venture into the specific passages on usury. These passages on usury are not just some obscure clobber passages, but rather, they fit neatly into the framework of other broad themes in scripture, of which usury is just one example.

Part 1: Usury in the Old Testament

Before we dive into the specific verses on usury, we should spend a moment explaining the different words you will see that are translated to either "interest," "usury," or "excessive interest" within the Bible. In the original Hebrew, the word for usury used most often is *"neshek,"* which comes from the word *"neshak,"* which means a biting, such as that of a serpent.[24] You will see this word translated to usury in the King James version written in 1611. In contrast, in newer translations, you will see this translated to either "interest" or sometimes "excessive interest." The English term usury is derived from the Latin *usuria*, relating to selling the use of property. Usury at the time of the King James translation meant what we now understand "interest" to mean - when a lender receives more than the amount loaned, he is paid back with interest. The shift from "usury" to "interest" was gradual from the early 17th century to today. Interest comes from the Latin word *interess,* meaning compensatory payments. Throughout the Middle Ages and the next few centuries, usury meant charging beyond the principal for a loan, which carried a distinctively negative connotation. However, in the early modern era and into our modern age, claims were made that in certain situations, the lender had an "interest" to receive

---

[24] S. C. Mooney, *Usury: Destroyer of Nations* (Warsaw: Theopolis, 1988), 2.

compensation beyond the principal, thus attempting to create the distinction between usury (bad lending) and interest (good lending). As public opinions on the matter continued to shift in favor of affirming these distinctions, someone today would most commonly understand the word "usury" to mean "excessive interest" along the lines of modern usury laws that ban interest at high amounts. Someone would most commonly understand "interest" to mean an amount received on a loan of money greater than the principal.

Now, I have no interest (pardon my pun) in squabbling over the language we use today for this discussion. As I stated earlier, I will use interest and usury interchangeably and use them both to mean any addition to the principal of an amount loaned. Whether we translate the word "*neshek*" to usury or interest only matters insofar as it correctly conveys the meaning at the time of the writing in its original language as closely as can be done in our current time in our modern language. There is little conceivable way to imagine that the writers of the Bible meant anything other than a loan where *any* amount greater than the amount loaned was received. It's a rather uncontroversial fact of history that usury (which was the word chosen for translation until the modern era) meant *any* amount of interest on a loan. The economic theories that attempted to parse distinctions between loans of usury and those of interest did not begin appearing until the Middle Ages, millennia after the original writings of the Bible.[25] So "*neshek*" can be translated to either usury or interest if one understands this means *any* interest on a loan; however, a translation of excessive interest simply does not accurately reflect the meaning of this term at the time of writing but rather reads in modern economic theories into the translation.

Now that we have covered that preamble, let's take a broad view as we consider the verses on usury and let the rather clear ones inform us first before getting to the tricky ones. I list these in detail, as we can lose sight of the forest from the trees if we look first at the unclear verses when several verses in many different contexts seem clear about denouncing usury without qualifications. For simplicity's sake, I will use the King James and New King James translations as these translate the original Hebrew words ("*neshek*" or "*mashsha*", meaning "exaction") and the Greek word (*tokos* used in the "Parable of the Talents") to usury.[26] I have also listed the Hebrew words translated to usury or increase in each of these

---

25 Mooney, *Destroyer of Nations*, 4-6.
26 Mooney, *Destroyer of Nations*, 100.

passages below.

<u>Usury unequivocally condemned:</u>

1. Psalm 15:1 & 15:5: "Lord, who may abide in Your tabernacle? Who may dwell in Your holy hill?…He *who* does not put out his money at *usury*, Nor does he take a bribe against the innocent. He who does these *things* shall never be moved."
    a. Usury is translated from the word, *neshek*, meaning a biting.
2. Nehemiah 5:1-11: "And there was a great outcry of the people and their wives against their Jewish brethren. For there were those who said, 'We, our sons, and our daughters are many; therefore let us get grain, that we may eat and live.' There were also some who said, 'We have mortgaged our lands and vineyards and houses, that we might buy grain because of the famine.' There were also those who said, 'We have borrowed money for the king's tax on our lands and vineyards. Yet now our flesh is as the flesh of our brethren, our children as their children; and indeed we are forcing our sons and our daughters to be slaves, and some of our daughters have been brought into slavery. It is not in our power to redeem them, for other men have our lands and vineyards.' After serious thought, I rebuked the nobles and rulers, and said to them, 'Each of you is exacting *usury* from his brother.' So I called a great assembly against them. And I said to them, 'According to our ability we have redeemed our Jewish brethren who were sold to the nations. Now indeed, will you even sell your brethren? Or should they be sold to us?' Then they were silenced and found nothing *to say.* Then I said, 'What you are doing *is* not good. Should you not walk in the fear of our God because of the reproach of the nations, our enemies? I also, *with* my brethren and my servants, am lending them money and grain. Please, let us stop this *usury*! Restore now to them, even this day, their lands, their vineyards, their olive groves, and their houses, also a hundredth of the money and the grain, the new wine and the oil, that you have charged them.'"
    a. Usury is translated from the word, *mashsha*, meaning "exaction."
3. Ezekiel 18:8-9: "'If he has not exacted usury nor taken any increase, But has withdrawn his hand from iniquity and executed true judgment between man and man; If he has walked in My statutes And kept My judgments faithfully— He is just; He shall

surely live!' Says the Lord God."
- a. Usury is translated from *neshek*, meaning "biting."
- b. Increase is translated from *tarbith*, meaning "an increase."
4. Ezekiel 18:13: "If he has exacted usury or taken increase—Shall he then live? He shall not live! If he has done any of these abominations, He shall surely die; His blood shall be upon him."
- a. Usury is translated from *neshek*, meaning "biting."
- b. Increase is translated from *tarbith*, meaning "an increase."
5. Ezekiel 18:17: "Who has withdrawn his hand from the poor and not received usury or increase, But has executed My judgments And walked in My statutes—He shall not die for the iniquity of his father; He shall surely live!"
- a. Usury is translated from *neshek*, meaning "biting."
- b. Increase is translated from *tarbith*, meaning "an increase."
6. Ezekiel 22:12: "In thee have they taken gifts to shed blood; thou hast taken usury and increase, and thou hast greedily gained of thy neighbours by extortion, and hast forgotten me, saith the Lord God."
- a. Usury is translated from *neshek*, meaning "biting."
- b. Increase is translated from *tarbith*, meaning "an increase."
7. Proverbs 28:8: "One who increases his possessions by usury and extortion gathers it for him who will pity the poor."
- a. Usury is translated from *neshek*, meaning "biting".
- b. Extortion is translated from the word *tarbith*, meaning "an increase."

In these verses above, you have a straightforward condemnation of usury on several occasions. In Psalm 15, the writer asks who may abide in God's tabernacle or dwell in His holy hill, and it states rather clearly that the one who lends at usury may not abide in God's tabernacle or dwell in His holy hill. In Nehemiah 5, Nehemiah becomes outraged upon learning that the Jewish people were charging interest to one another and demands that every amount be restored to the hundredth of the money and the grain. Nehemiah also affirms the idea of lending in general as he is lending *with* them but condemns their lending at usury. In Ezekiel, there are multiple situations where the one who does not exact usury is just, whereas the one who has exacted usury has committed abominations. In Proverbs, you have the idea stated rather clearly that the one who commits usury is not gracious to the poor, and it hints at the sovereign justice of God that will, in the long run, result in true riches for tho just man even though the wicked may materially prosper temporarily in this life. These verses are about as straightforward as it gets - the usurer, the one who lends at interest, is stated to have committed abominations, will not dwell in God's tabernacle, and should restore down to the hundredth the amount of money received from usury.

For those who claim scripture is authoritative over their lives and yet think nothing of the sinfulness of interest, you will rarely hear them quote the verses above. You will, however, often hear some argument that usury, or charging interest, is only a sin insofar as it is done to the poor. Let us examine these verses next.

Usury only applicable to "The Poor" verses:

1. Leviticus: 25:35-37: "And if thy brother be waxen poor, and fallen in decay with thee; then thou shalt relieve him: yea, though he be a stranger, or a sojourner; that he may live with thee. Take thou no usury of him, or increase: but fear thy God; that thy brother may live with thee. Thou shalt not give him thy money upon usury, nor lend him thy victuals for increase."
   a. Usury is translated from *neshek*, meaning "biting."
   b. Increase is translated from *tarbith*, meaning "an increase."
2. Exodus 22:25: "If thou lend money to any of my people that is poor by thee, thou shalt not be to him as an usurer, neither shalt thou lay upon him usury."
   a. Usury is translated from *neshek*, meaning "biting."

All these verses say is do not lend at usury to the poor - nothing more and nothing less. It says nothing about those who are not poor. Why should we automatically assume that just because I am told not to do something to a poor person, I should do it to someone who is not poor? If I am told not to oppress a widowed woman or an orphan child, ought I to conclude that I am being instructed to oppress a married man? Of course not - this would be absurd. And yet, if we applied the same logic we do to the usury prohibition of the poor, we would use Exodus 22:22 to argue that we ought to oppress married men (Exodus 22:25: "Ye shall not afflict any widow, or fatherless child."). If I am told not to rape a woman, I do not assume that I should rape a man; it just happens to be that women are more often than men to be in vulnerable positions at risk of rape such that a command may be more likely to be given specifically to these situations. Such is the case with the poor and usury. The poor are most likely to need a loan, so the reminder is not to lend at usury to the poor.

Now, if these were the only verses in the Bible relating to lending at interest and they only spoke specifically of lending to the poor, then I could understand the argument to make the qualification that usury is only a sin when lending to the poor; however, we have already reviewed several verses that condemned usury in general terms, not specific to the poor, and now we are looking at verses that condemn it specifically for the poor. If you have a general condemnation and a specific condemnation, then the obvious interpretation would be to maintain the general condemnation, not to think the specific condemnation with no reference to the morality of lending outside of the specific condemnation could somehow override the general condemnation. This is absurd logic. If you look at verses that clearly say *don't lend at usury* with no qualifications, and then some that simply say *don't lend at usury to the poor*, there is no reason to conclude that we should be able to lend at usury to those that are not poor.

Usury not intrinsically sinful verses:
Ah, but one might point to Deuteronomy 23:19-20 and say that usury can't be intrinsically harmful or sinful given that God commands it.

- Deuteronomy 23:19-20: "You shall not charge interest to your brother (*ach*)—interest on money *or* food *or* anything that is lent out at interest. To a foreigner (*nokri*) you may charge interest, but to your brother (*ach*) you shall not charge interest, that the Lord your God may bless you in all to which you set your hand in the land which you are entering to possess."

In the recently released and quite popular book, *The New Confessions of an Economic Hit Man*, there's a telling quote where the author, John Perkins, lays out quite bluntly the purpose he was told for his job as an economic hit man: "...there were two primary objectives of my work. First, I was to justify huge international loans that would funnel money back to MAIN and other US companies... through massive engineering and construction projects. Second, I would work to bankrupt the countries that received those loans (after they had paid MAIN and the other US contractors, of course), so that they would be forever beholden to their creditors and would present easy targets when we needed favors, such as military bases, UN votes, or access to oil and other natural resources."[27] Such is the situation we are dealing with in these verses - this speaks to economic warfare, not some justification to usury not being harmful.

Let's first notice the last phrase of this passage, *"that the Lord your God may bless you in all to which you set your hand in the land which you are entering to possess."* A careful reader of Deuteronomy may notice this phrase appears exactly as written in this verse multiple times earlier in this book as well, and there are several variations of this instruction throughout the Torah. For just one example, in the beginning of Deuteronomy chapter 7 it says, "When the Lord your God brings you *into the land you are entering to possess* and drives out before you many nations—the Hittites, Girgashites, Amorites, Canaanites, Perizzites, Hivites and Jebusites, seven nations larger and stronger than you— and when the Lord your God has delivered them over to you and you have defeated them, then you must destroy them totally. Make no treaty with them, and show them no mercy." Further to the point, Deuteronomy 7:22-23 says "The Lord your God will drive out those nations before you, little by little. You will not be allowed to eliminate them all at once, or the wild animals will multiply around you. But the Lord your God will deliver them over to you, throwing them into great confusion until they are destroyed" It seems rather intuitive that a form of economic warfare in the form of crippling usury could be a part of a more comprehensive war strategy for the Lord to bless the Israelites in the land they are entering to possess, such that the nations are driven out little by little, not all at once. Now, I understand these verses of commanded destruction in the Hebrew scriptures can bring up some tricky theological questions that are well beyond the scope of this work; however, as it relates to usury, these commands of destruction of the individuals currently inhabiting *the land you are entering to possess* are further confirmation of the inherent harmfulness of usury, where use should be restricted to the rarest of circumstances. Usury is much like killing - it is always harmful to the other, but in rare circumstances such as self-defense or a just war situation, the killing of another is

[27] John Perkins, *The New Confessions of an Economic Hit Man* (Oakland: Berrett-Koehler Publishers, 2016), 27.

still quite obviously harmful, but yet not murder or sinful.

To further bring this point home, we should look deeper into the translation of the word foreigner in verse 20. There are two Hebrew words for foreigner - *ger* and *nokri*. *Ger* is essentially what we would think of as something like an immigrant, whereas *nokri* always has explicitly negative connotations associated with it. *Nokri* is the word used to describe the adultress in Proverbs, and it is also used throughout Deuteronomy and Leviticus separately from *ger*, with instructions on how to treat a *ger* differing quite sharply from the instructions on how to treat a *nokri*. The commands for how to treat a German immigrant in the United States in the 21st century (something like a *ger*) would be quite different from the commands of how to treat a Nazi solider during World War II (something like a *nokri*).[28]

If you read these verses with those contexts in mind, then it becomes clear that the only time usury is justified throughout all of scripture is in context to a word used to describe an evil and hostile people *in the land which you are entering to possess.* This is instructing economic warfare in a narrow sense in the lands Israel is entering to possess in a similar vein to the verses throughout the Torah where the Israelites are commanded to destroy the Hittites, etc.

Part 2: Usury in the New Testament

So, in summary so far, within the Bible, you have high-level themes repeatedly warning Israel in the Old Testament and the early church in the New Testament of idolatry and greed, you have several passages condemning usury as an abomination in a general sense, you have specific passages condemning usury to the poor, and you have a verse saying don't lend at usury, except to the *nokri in the land which you are entering to possess* in the manner of similar passages within Deuteronomy commanding the total destruction of the inhabitants *in the land which you are entering to possess.* This seems increasingly straightforward.

Parable of the Talents:

---

[28] Mooney, *Destroyer of Nations*, 148.

Ah, but one might say, what about the Parable of the Talents? Doesn't Jesus say that usury is not only okay but encouraged? Let's take a look at the version in the Gospel of Luke and see. I encourage you to read this parable in its entirety.

Luke 19:11-27[29]: "While they were listening to this, he went on to tell them a parable, because he was near Jerusalem and the people thought that the kingdom of God was going to appear at once. He said: 'A man of noble birth went to a distant country to have himself appointed king and then to return. So he called ten of his servants and gave them ten minas. 'Put this money to work,' he said, 'until I come back.' But his subjects hated him and sent a delegation after him to say, 'We don't want this man to be our king.' He was made king, however, and returned home. Then he sent for the servants to whom he had given the money, in order to find out what they had gained with it. The first one came and said, 'Sir, your mina has earned ten more.' Well done, my good servant!' his master replied. 'Because you have been trustworthy in a very small matter, take charge of ten cities.' The second came and said, 'Sir, your mina has earned five more.' His master answered, 'You take charge of five cities.' Then another servant came and said, 'Sir, here is your mina; I have kept it laid away in a piece of cloth. I was afraid of you, because you are a hard man. You take out what you did not put in and reap what you did not sow.' His master replied, 'I will judge you by your own words, you wicked servant! You knew, did you, that I am a hard man, taking out what I did not put in, and reaping what I did not sow? Why then didn't you put my money on deposit, so that when I came back, I could have collected it with interest?' Then he said to those standing by, 'Take his mina away from him and give it to the one who has ten minas.' 'Sir,' they said, 'he already has ten!' He replied, 'I tell you that to everyone who has, more will be given, but as for the one who has nothing, even what they have will be taken away. But those enemies of mine who did not want me to be king over them—bring them here and kill them in front of me.'"

Now re-read verses 20-23:

"Then another servant came and said, 'Sir, here is your mina; I have kept it laid away in a piece of cloth. I was afraid of you, because you are a hard man. You take out what you did not put in and reap what you did not sow.' His master replied, 'I will judge you by your own

---

[29] *English Standard Version.*

words, you wicked servant! You knew, did you, that I am a hard man, taking out what I did not put in, and reaping what I did not sow? Why then didn't you put my money on deposit, so that when I came back, I could have collected it with interest?'"

It's right there in front of you - do you see it? The lazy servant who hides his mina claims that he does so because the master is a "hard man," and the lazy servant claims that the master takes out what he did not put in and reaps what he does not sow. The master replies, 'I will judge you by your own words, you wicked servant! You knew, did you, that I am a hard man, taking out what I did not put in, and reaping what I did not sow? Why then didn't you put my money on deposit, so that when I came back, I could have collected it with interest?'"

Jesus has the master in this parable say quite literally His point of encouraging the wicked servant to put his money on deposit to lend at interest - it is to use the lazy servant's own words against him. *If* the lazy servant believed that his master was a hard man who reaped what he did not sow, *then* he would have lent at usury such that the master could have reaped what he did not sow by collecting upon his deposit with interest. This parable does not encourage lending at interest. But, rather it's perhaps an even more obvious condemnation of usury as Jesus Himself directly equates receiving money at interest with "taking out what [one] does not put in, and reaping what [one] does not sow." He uses this example to judge the lazy servant by his own words.

Out of all the biblical examples relating to usury where we completely overlook the truth, our reaction to this parable befuddles me perhaps more than any other. Most of the other verses are safely tucked away in the chapters of the Law and the Prophets, which, just like our old yearbooks or boxes of childhood photographs, we like the idea of having them available to us much more than the reality of looking through them. But this is right there in the gospels, front and center!

The nearly universal interpretation of this parable as it relates to interest is to consider Jesus as suggesting that the lazy servant should have at least invested his money to get some monetary return, almost as a further condemnation of his unwillingness to take any sort of risk. This common interpretation is exemplified in *The Message* paraphrase of the Bible of Luke 19:22-23: "He said,

'You're right that I don't suffer fools gladly—and you've acted the fool! Why didn't you at least invest the money in securities so I would have gotten a little interest on it?'"[30] I offer this example not to disparage *The Message* translation or its author, as he's an author and pastor whom I tremendously respect and whose writings have benefited me immensely, but simply because it succinctly summarizes the most common interpretation.

However, this interpretation is simply not slowing down to read what is written, and instead thinking you already know the answer before reading the text. On the one hand, I get it - it's like one of those riddles where our intuitive "system 1" brain jumps to an answer that seems plausible without ever engaging our slow and thoughtful "system 2" intellect to think critically through a problem. For example, Kate's mother has three children: Snap, Crackle, and ___. Who's the third child?[31] Or "A bat and a ball cost $1.10 in total. The bat costs $1.00 more than the ball. How much does the ball cost? _____ cents"[32] These are obvious answers when you stop and think through them, yet most of us will miss them. But on the other hand, imagine the sheer volume of times that the "Parable of the Talents," or the "Parable of the Minas," has been read over the last few centuries by believers and unbelievers - probably millions, or perhaps even billions of times. Yet, we are all so entrenched in the secular ideologies and monetary systems of our day that entire generations can completely gloss over what the text says, as we are convinced we already know what it means. How many times have I done this myself?! How often do I still do this in other areas I am completely blind to? Lord, give us "eyes to see and ears to hear!"

Lend expecting nothing in return:
And last, but certainly not least, just so we have no excuse not to understand the truth about the sinfulness of lending at interest, we have Jesus Himself directly imploring His disciples to "lend, expecting nothing in return" (Luke 6:35).[33]

Jesus says in the verse immediately preceding 6:35 "Even sinners lend to sinners, to get back the same amount." Therefore, it seems

---

[30] Eugene Peterson, *The Message* (Colorado Springs: NavPress, 2017).
[31] It's not "Pop," it's Kate
[32] Daniel Kahneman, *Thinking, Fast and Slow* (New York: Farrar, Straus and Giroux, 2011), 44. As Daniel Kahneman's famous studies show, more than half of respondents to surveys have been recorded as saying 10 cents, although this is not correct as this would equal $1.20 total ($.10 + $1.10 = $1.20). The ball costs 5 cents ($.05 + $1.05 = $1.10)
[33] *English Standard Version*.

most likely that Jesus is imploring us to go beyond the expectation to simply lend to others and expect to receive back what we lent and instead to lend in situations where we would not expect to even receive our principal back. But even if one does not take this command to go as far as not to expect your principal back, I certainly cannot imagine how one reads this verse and imagines it does not at least preclude lending expecting *more* than what you lent in return.

So again, in summary, you have warnings against the danger of money and idolatry throughout the Bible, you have verses in the Law and Prophets that condemn or forbid usury without equivocation, you have verses that forbid usury to the poor in the Torah, you have verses in Deuteronomy that forbid usury to a brother but allow usury to the enemies of Israel that they are instructed to destroy totally, "in the land they are entering to possess," you have Jesus referencing the idea of usury as equivalent to one who "reaps where he does not sow" and "taking out what he does not put in," and you have Jesus Himself commanding that His disciples "lend expecting nothing in return."

Part 3: The Law

I believe there's a coherence in how these passages relate together that I will do my best to explain in hopes that it may benefit the reader. Still, to do so, there's no way around the reality that I will be traversing heavily debated doctrines and scriptural interpretations that have gone on for millennia surrounding how "the Law" relates to Christians today. I will try to sidestep controversies unrelated to usury where I can, but undoubtedly, I will assume some positions on theological matters still hotly in dispute by many. However, even in instances where one may disagree with me as it relates to how Christians should understand "the Law" after the death and resurrection of Jesus Christ, I submit that the scriptural arguments condemning usury would still hold within any Christian theology that takes the authority of scripture seriously. Since you have Jesus, Himself saying, "lend, expecting nothing in return"[34] and using usury as the negative example of behavior in the Parable of the Talents, even the most ardent Marcionite cannot honestly avoid facing the uncomfortable truth of usury. The only Christian theological frameworks that I think could coherently ignore usury condemnation

---

[34] Luke 10:35.

would be those extreme versions of antinomianism, where you excuse any sinful behavior in yourself that you want and avoid taking any commands from God seriously that are inconvenient to you, hoping that God's grace will cover these sins even without any serious effort at repentance. There are, of course, numerous warnings about this sort of gleeful disregard for holiness throughout Paul's letters ("What shall we say then? Are we to continue in sin that grace may abound? By no means! How can we who died to sin still live in it?" (Romans 6:1-2)), and with Christ's words Himself ("Not everyone who cries out "Lord, Lord" will enter the kingdom of heaven" (Matthew 7:21)).

So, with that preamble out of the way, here's how I understand these passages to relate to us today regarding the sinfulness of lending at interest, starting "In the beginning" (Genesis 1:1). God made man and woman and gave them but one command - "You are free to eat from any tree in the garden; but you must not eat from the tree of the knowledge of good and evil, for when you eat from it you will certainly die" (Genesis 2:16-17). And yet Adam and Eve both disobeyed God, willfully separating humanity from the Author of Creation, and as a result, we must suffer the wages of sin, which is death.

Here, you have the first examples of the Law, the blueprint for how humans are to live to achieve the pinnacle of flourishing meant for humanity, and the first consequences of failing to adhere to this blueprint for how we ought to live. When I refer to the Law, this can include what is commonly referred to as *natural law*, or those aspects of the way humanity ought to act "for the common good" that can be understood purely through reason, and *divine law*, those instructions relating to the Law that are revealed to us specifically by God Himself. It should also be noted that while natural law and divine law are the best guides for us as they are intelligible to humans, they are reflections of the *eternal law*. "For now we see only a reflection as in a mirror; then we shall see face to face. Now I know in part; then I shall know fully, even as I am fully known" (1 Corinthians 13:12).

So following in the tradition of Aquinas, you have the eternal law that emanates from the nature of God Himself before[35] and separate from the confines of time and is a sort of intelligence that is directing

---

[35] *New Advent*, Aquinas, *Summa Theologiae*, First Part of the Second Part, Question 93, https://www.newadvent.org/summa/2093.htm

all beings to their "due end." This eternal law is much too holy for us to directly encounter in this life (much like how the unfiltered rays of the sun would consume us if we were too close). You have the reflection of this universal, unchanging Law manifesting itself upon humanity based on the unique conditions in history through the *natural law* and *divine law*. Through reason alone, you have examples such as Confucius discovering the natural law principle of "Do not impose on others what you do not wish for yourself." Through instructions revealed directly by God, you have divine law examples in the Garden of Eden ("don't eat the fruit"), and perhaps the most famous divine law example with the collection of laws given to Moses and the Israelites and recorded within the first five books of the Bible that are commonly referred to as "the Old Law" or "the Mosaic Law," among other names.

Within the Mosaic Law, there is quite an assortment of commands, often described as numbering 613 in total. Within these different commandments, a common distinction is made to separate these laws into three different types - "moral law," "judicial law," and "ceremonial law." The moral law refers to those laws that are universally obligatory at all times and places, and per Aquinas,[36] includes those that are obvious to all (e.g., "thou shalt not steal"), those that are equally obligatory but require more careful consideration from wise men to discern (e.g., "Stand up in the presence of the aged, show respect for the elderly and revere your God."), and those that require divine instruction to know ("Thou shalt not make to thyself a graven thing, nor the likeness of anything; Thou shalt not take the name of the Lord thy God in vain"). The judicial law refers to laws binding under the particular theocratic government of Israel at that time relating to human relations with other humans (e.g., "When a man is newly married, he shall not go out with the army or be liable for any other public duty. He shall be free at home one year to be happy with his wife whom he has taken" (Deuteronomy 24:5)). The ceremonial law refers to man's subordination to God and the instructions relating to proper worship of God given to Moses and the Israelites (e.g., "When anyone brings a grain offering as an offering to the Lord, his offering shall be of fine flour. He shall pour oil on it and put frankincense on it" (Leviticus 2:1)).

And finally, you have what is commonly called "the New Law,"

---

[36] *New Advent*, Aquinas, *Summa Theologiae,* First Part of the Second Part, Question 100, https://www.newadvent.org/summa/2100.htm#article1

which, as Aquinas puts it, "is chiefly the grace itself of the Holy Ghost, which is given to those who believe in Christ."[37] The following reference within the book of Jeremiah and by the writer of Hebrews also refers to this Law written on our hearts: "This is the covenant that I will make with them after those days, declares the Lord: I will put my laws on their hearts, and write them on their minds" (Hebrews 10:16).

So, as it relates to the Law in the most general sense, every single human being who reaches an age to be able to reason (leaving aside questions around infants, etc.) has been given adequate information to have some knowledge of at least the *natural* law.

"For the wrath of God is revealed from heaven against all ungodliness and unrighteousness of men, who by their unrighteousness suppress the truth. For what can be known about God is plain to them, because God has shown it to them. For his invisible attributes, namely, his eternal power and divine nature, have been clearly perceived, ever since the creation of the world, in the things that have been made. So, they are without excuse" (Romans 1:18-20).

"Indeed, when Gentiles, who do not have the law, do by nature things required by the law, they are a law for themselves, even though they do not have the law. They show that the requirements of the law are written on their hearts, their consciences also bearing witness, and their thoughts sometimes accusing them and at other times even defending them" (Romans 2:14-15).

Now, the Law (in the most general sense) will be provided and articulated to varying levels of clarity to different individuals and people groups today and throughout history, with the most direct articulation being provided to the Israelites through the Torah. "Then what advantage has the Jew? Or what is the value of circumcision? Much in every way. To begin with, the Jews were entrusted with the oracles of God" (Romans 3:1-2). And yet, no matter whether we have only received slivers of the Law (e.g., if we only knew to do unto others as you would have them do unto you) or if we are the most learned religious scholar in the Torah or Bible, every single one of us fails to obey the Law, even though following the Law leads to our good. We always fail. And just like a car running 100,000

---

[37] *New Advent*, Thomas Aquinas, *Summa Theologica,* First Part of the Second Part, Question 106, Article 1, https://www.newadvent.org/summa/2106.htm

miles without an oil change, the results are catastrophic. "Now we know that whatever the law says it speaks to those who are under the law, so that every mouth may be stopped, and the whole world may be held accountable to God. For by works of the law no human being will be justified in his sight, since through the law comes knowledge of sin" (Romans 3:19-20).

An honest assessment of one's condition reveals our helplessness before God - we know what's good, and yet we do what's bad, and we're deserving of death and eternal punishment. And yet "God so loved the world that He sent His only Son that whoever believes would not perish but have eternal life" (John 3:16). By trusting in Christ, we "are justified by his grace as a gift, through the redemption that is in Christ Jesus, whom God put forward as a propitiation by his blood, to be received by faith" (Romans 3:23-24).

So please do not misunderstand anything I am writing to suggest anything other than the gospel - the good news that Christ died for our sins. "For we hold that one is justified by faith apart from works of the law" (Romans 3:28). But - "Do we then overthrow the law by this faith? By no means! On the contrary, we uphold the law" (Romans 3:31).

The Law in the most general sense, whether referring to natural law or any divine law such as the Mosaic Law, is for the benefit of its recipients. Chesterton speaks of the freedom that comes from the Law by comparing it to children's freedom when constraints produce a field safely partitioned for frolicking. "We might fancy some children playing on the flat grassy top of some tall island in the sea. So long as there was a wall round the cliff's edge they could fling themselves into every frantic game and make the place the noisiest of nurseries. But the walls were broken down, leaving the naked peril of the precipice. They did not fall over; but when their friends returned to them they were all huddled in terror in the centre of the island; and their song had ceased."[38] The Law, if properly and universally understood and followed, would produce a society of whimsical bliss, with an infinite number of possibilities for joy and love and creativity within the constraints designed to nurture human flourishing. The Law is good, not bad. And please do not just take my word for it, scripture plainly reveals this to be true:

---

[38] G. K. Chesterton, *Orthodoxy* (1934).

- "The law of the Lord is perfect, reviving the soul; the testimony of the Lord is sure, making wise the simple" (Psalm 19:7)[39]
- "And what great nation is there, that has statutes and rules so righteous as all this law that I set before you today?" (Deuteronomy 4:8).[40]
- "So the law is holy, and the commandment is holy and righteous and good" (Romans 7:12)[41]

So, the Law is good, and the Law did not go away with Jesus. Jesus did not come to abolish "the Law" but to fulfill it. "Do not think that I have come to abolish the Law or the Prophets; I have not come to abolish them but to fulfill them. For truly, I say to you, until heaven and earth pass away, not an iota, not a dot, will pass from the Law until all is accomplished. Therefore, whoever relaxes one of the least of these commandments and teaches others to do the same will be called least in the kingdom of heaven, but whoever does them and teaches them will be called great in the kingdom of heaven" (Matthew 5:17-19).[42]

While the Law contains numerous curses detailed in Deuteronomy 27 & 28 for those who do not adhere to it, the Law itself is not a curse. All who rely on works under the Law are under a curse because all fall short of adhering to the Law's requirements and, therefore, are under condemnation based on its stipulations. Still, the Law itself is not the curse; rather, those under the Law dependent on works are cursed by the Law. Therefore, Christ redeemed us from the curse of the consequences of the Law by becoming a curse on our behalf. "For all who rely on works of the law are under a curse; for it is written, "Cursed be everyone who does not abide by all things written in the Book of the Law, and do them." Christ redeemed us from the curse of the Law by becoming a curse for us—for it is written, "Cursed is everyone who is hanged on a tree" (Galatians 3:10-13).[43]

Part 4: Usury and The Law

So, the Law is good, Jesus did not abolish the Law, and the Law is

---

[39] *English Standard Version.*
[40] *English Standard Version.*
[41] *English Standard Version.*
[42] *English Standard Version.*
[43] *English Standard Version.*

not a curse. Yet, there is still some rather complicated discernment as it relates to applying instructions from the Torah to our lives today. Most would agree that avoiding killing one's neighbor remains wise today, but few seem to be out killing rams and splattering blood on a temple that no longer exists (which, by the way, I do not think we should be doing today). But why is this? Who are we to pick and choose what rules apply and when and how does this apply to usury? Well, here's how I understand the matter.

The Old Law, or the Mosaic Law, includes three components I summarized earlier - the moral law, which is universal, the judicial law, which applied specifically to the theocratic society of Israel, and the ceremonial law, which relates to proper worship of God.

Let's take the ceremonial law first. The ceremonial law includes a litany of instructions regarding proper worship, such as what to wear, what to sacrifice, how the temple should be constructed, the different roles of the priests, etc. As an oversimplification, both on Mount Sinai and within the Tabernacle, there are increasing levels of holiness the further you get into the core of the worship space. For example, those in the Outer Courtyard are in a less holy space than those in the Holy Place, and anything in the Holy of Holies is obviously in the holiest space of all. To be fit to cross these thresholds into holy spaces, there was typically some combination of two things that needed to happen - you needed to be cleansed with water, and an animal needed to be sacrificed. Blood and water were required. However, Jesus has now fulfilled these ceremonial law requirements for us hence they are no longer required.

Cleansing could be required of the priests before religious ceremonies ("He is to put on the sacred linen tunic, with linen undergarments next to his body; he is to tie the linen sash around him and put on the linen turban. These are sacred garments; so he must bathe himself with water before he puts them on." (Leviticus 16:4)), or cleansing could be required of individuals with skin diseases prior to them being fit to return into the fabric of the society ("The priest is to go outside the camp and examine them. If they have been healed of their defiling skin disease, the priest shall order that two live clean birds and some cedar wood, scarlet yarn and hyssop be brought for the person to be cleansed" (Leviticus 14:3-4)).

Oftentimes cleansing would be required from a running water

stream, or what was referred to as living water ("'And when he who has a discharge is cleansed of his discharge, then he shall count for himself seven days for his cleansing, wash his clothes, and bathe his body in *running* water; then he shall be clean." (Leviticus 15:13)[44], whereas now Jesus freely offers us this "living water" - "If you knew the gift of God and who it is that asks you for a drink, you would have asked him and he would have given you living water" (John 4:10).

Of course, there are numerous examples of blood sacrifices throughout Leviticus, where the priests perform different animal sacrifices for the forgiveness of sins. "And do with this bull just as he did with the bull for the sin offering. In this way, the priest will make atonement for the community, and they will be forgiven" (Leviticus 4:20).

While these sacrifices were offered for the forgiveness of sins, these sacrifices were but shadows of the ultimate reality and greater sacrifice that would eventually be offered for us through Jesus Christ. "The law is only a shadow of the good things that are coming—not the realities themselves. For this reason it can never, by the same sacrifices repeated endlessly year after year, make perfect those who draw near to worship. Otherwise, would they not have stopped being offered? For the worshipers would have been cleansed once for all, and would no longer have felt guilty for their sins. But those sacrifices are an annual reminder of sins. It is impossible for the blood of bulls and goats to take away sins" (Hebrews 10:1-4). The blood of Jesus, in His own words, "is my blood of the covenant, which is poured out for many for the forgiveness of sins" (Matthew 26:27-28).

As a further reminder of Jesus serving as our living water to prepare us fit to encounter the holiness of God and the blood sacrifice needed to atone for our sins, you have evidence after Christ's death as His side was pierced. This cleansing water and atoning blood gushed forth from His body - "But one of the soldiers pierced his side with a spear, and at once there came out blood and water" (John 19:34).[45]

Hallelujah - what a savior! Through the blood and cleansing of Christ "let us draw near to God with a sincere heart and with the full

---

[44] *New King James Version.*
[45] *English Standard Version.*

assurance that faith brings, having our *hearts sprinkled to cleanse us* from a guilty conscience and having our bodies *washed with pure water*" (Hebrews 10:20-22).

So, the ceremonial law was not necessarily *abolished* - we still require forgiveness for our sins and cleansing before being fit to encounter God - Jesus just *fulfilled* these requirements on our behalf. Therefore, we are no longer to rely on the priestly sacrifices of animals and cleansing rituals that are mere shadows compared to the reality of the cleansing and sacrifice that Jesus offers. "But when Christ came as high priest of the good things that are now already here, he went through the greater and more perfect tabernacle that is not made with human hands, that is to say, is not a part of this creation. He did not enter by means of the blood of goats and calves; but he entered the Most Holy Place once for all by his own blood, thus obtaining eternal redemption" (Hebrews 9:11-12).

Now, onto the judicial law. I think Aquinas succinctly articulates why the judicial law is no longer binding on us today. "The judicial precepts established by men retain their binding force for ever, so long as the state of government remains the same. But if the state or nation pass to another form of government, the laws must needs be changed. For democracy, which is government by the people, demands different laws from those of oligarchy, which is government by the rich, as the Philosopher shows. Consequently, when the state of that people changed, the judicial precepts had to be changed also."[46] The judicial laws were instructions given to people living in the theocratic nation of Israel, and they were binding under the authority of that particular government. As the government changes, the judicial statutes of that new government will be the new binding laws for the subjects of that government, assuming, of course, that the judicial laws of the government do not contradict greater laws of God. While the spirit and themes behind the judicial laws are still quite informative as to what God considers a just society, the judicial laws themselves are no longer binding on us today as we are under a different system of government.

This brings us back to the moral law examples contained within the Mosaic law, especially how one who trusts in Jesus Christ as their Savior should respond to these moral commandments. On the one hand, you have instructions that seem to suggest we should just

---

[46] *New Advent,* Thomas Aquinas, *Summa Theologica,* First Part of the Second Part, Question 104, Article 3, Reply to Objection 2, https://www.newadvent.org/summa/2104.htm

blatantly ignore these moral commands, such as this passage in Galatians: "Before the coming of this faith, we were held in custody under the law, locked up until the faith that was to come would be revealed. So, the law was our guardian until Christ came that we might be justified by faith. Now that this faith has come, we are no longer under a guardian" (Galatians 3:23-25). If we are no longer under the guardianship of the Law, why should we care what it has to say?

But then you have Jesus directly saying, "I did not come to abolish the Law and the Prophets," and you have Paul in Romans directly saying ,"Do we, then, nullify the law by this faith? Not at all! Rather, we uphold the law" (Romans 3:31). These sure make it seem like we should be upholding these moral commandments. What are we to make of this?

Much of the complexity relates to the same word "law" (or "nomos" in Greek) being used in many different contexts, some of which were explained above. This word can mean the natural law, divine law, the Mosaic law, Halakha (the oral tradition of Jewish Laws expounding on the Torah laws), or laws of a particular country, just to name a few. So, depending on one's interpretation of the meaning of the word "law" used in a particular context, one can come up with different interpretations. While this may seem hopelessly confusing, the practical implications of the different interpretations of how believers should treat the moral law are usually not that different. We usually find similar answers, even though the approach may differ.

To elaborate on this further, we must best try to understand the relationship of the "Old Law" with the "New Law". We have already discussed the distinction between how the Old Law is like a shadow compared to the ultimate and greater reality of the New Covenant as it relates to Jesus being able to fully atone for sins on our behalf in a way that could not be accomplished under the Old Law. Additionally, the New Law is "chiefly the grace itself of the Holy Ghost, which is given to those who believe in Christ,"[47] as Aquinas puts it. This New Law is "put in our hearts and written on our minds,"[48] and the grace that transforms our minds to perceive the spirit of the law is also the same grace that transforms us into

---

[47] New Advent, Thomas Aquinas, Summa Theologica, First Part of the Second Part, Question 106, Article 1, https://www.newadvent.org/summa/2106.htm
[48] Hebrews 10:16, English Standard Version.

creatures who increasingly desire to live out the spirit of the law out of obedience to God. There are also two other key distinctions between the New Covenant and the Old Law that are worth pointing out - 1) the Old Law focuses primarily on actions or external behaviors, whereas the New Law also focuses on the internal disposition, or what is commonly referred to as "the heart" behind our behaviors, and 2) the Old Law includes baseline expectations for behavior, whereas the New Covenant often extends these expectations to greater lengths than what was outlined in the Torah.

One of the most common examples of the 1st distinction is where murder is condemned in the Torah, and yet in the Sermon on the Mount, Jesus explains that even harboring anger towards another will warrant judgment (Matthew 5:21-22). You have a similar theme as it relates to adultery - the Torah expectation was not to have sex with someone who is not your spouse. In contrast, Jesus expounds this more fully to say you should not even lust after someone who is not your spouse as this is also adultery (Matthew 5:27-28).

A common example of the 2nd distinction (where the New Covenant extends the expectation of the Torah) is the "turn the other cheek" command. In the Torah, the "eye for an eye" expectation was a restraint on vengeance, which meant that retribution should be commensurate with the harm that was afflicted, not greater than the harm inflicted. Still, in the New Covenant, this is extended even further as Jesus expounds that if someone slaps you on the right cheek (meaning it would have been an especially offensive backhanded slap), you should not retaliate but rather turn the other cheek.

In the New Covenant, the one referenced in Jeremiah as being "in their minds" and "written on their hearts,"[49] you have this expectation being clarified of living out the spirit of the law and not just the letter of the law, with the spirit of the law often extending the baseline expectation of the Old Covenant and also considering the internal disposition and not just the external actions. Or as Paul puts it, "But now, by dying to what once bound us, we have been released from the law so that we serve in the new way of the Spirit, and not in the old way of the written code" (Romans 7:6).

---

[49] Jeremiah 31:33.

Part 5: If You Love Me, Keep My Commands

So, back to the question "what should a believer do with the moral law commands in the Torah?" Some will say we're not obligated to follow them, but they should inform our behavior (heavily emphasizing that we're not under the guardianship of the Law). Others will say we are still obligated to follow them (heavily emphasizing Matthew 5:17-19 and Paul's commands to follow the Law). However, the practical implications for sincere believers should usually end up in a similar place. Let's say we must still follow the moral precepts in the Old Covenant, then we admit to their continued validity. But, if we say we don't have to follow them, yet we admit the New Covenant has greater expectations on behavior than the Old Covenant as it relates to morality and love, then a sincere effort to live out the grace we have been shown by God in obedience to the New Covenant would require following the expectations of the moral law in the Old Covenant anyway. If we don't even lust (expectations of the spirit of the law), we obviously won't stray outside our marriage (expectations of the Old Covenant).

I have found Aquinas to articulate the distinctions between the Old Law and the New Law as helpful as anyone I can find. As a paraphrase for how Aquinas puts it, things determined for a purpose can be different in two ways - 1st - if they are seeking different ends or purposes, and 2nd - if they are closely or more remotely connected to the ultimate purpose. The New Law and the Old Law both have the same purpose - man's subjection to God - but the Old Law is like the elementary school lesson, whereas the New Law is like the graduate class.[50]

If the Old Law teaches basic arithmetic and you are moving on to advanced algebra and calculus, this assumes you can at least do your basic arithmetic. You can get your basic arithmetic correct and fail to be doing algebra or calculus correctly, but if you think you are doing algebra and calculus, and yet you are making errors with 2+2 then you are deceiving yourself if you think your advanced math equations are correct.

---

[50] Thomas Aquinas, *Summa Theologica*, First Part of the Second Part, Question 107, Article 1.

The Old Law and the New Law are imperfect compared to perfect. This use of imperfect does not mean bad, but rather not yet reaching its full maturity. So, a seed could be considered imperfect until it reaches its full stage of maturity in a tree, but that does not mean it is a bad seed.

The moral law examples in the Torah still matter as these are often just elementary school lessons of the Law. Jesus, however, points deeper to the heart behind the elementary school lessons with a sort of graduate course in moral law. We cannot ignore the elementary school lessons—those are supposed to be the easy ones—and without those, we certainly have no hope of achieving success in graduate courses.

As it relates to usury, the examples of usury prohibition or condemnation in the Old Testament relate to moral law examples. They are clearly not examples of ceremonial law and do not fit the judicial or civil law theme either. Civil law examples would read much like our modern laws, where an action is described, and a societal or justice system responds to those actions. For example, in our legal system, if you steal greater than a certain amount, you'll be charged with a felony, and if you steal a smaller amount, you'll be charged with a misdemeanor. In the Torah, you have an example: "Whoever steals an ox or a sheep and slaughters it or sells it must pay back five head of cattle for the ox and four sheep for the sheep" (Exodus 22:1).

However, each of the prohibitions on usury does not read like a civil law where they say what the judicial response should be in instances of usury; they just say don't do it, much like a "thou shalt not murder" command. Further to the point, within Psalm 15, the one who may dwell on the holy hill of the Lord is said to not lend at interest, along with several other examples such as the one "who does what is righteous, who speaks the truth from their heart; whose tongue utters no slander, who does no wrong to a neighbor, and casts no slur on others."[51] In this Psalm, the behavior of not lending at interest is lumped together with other behaviors, such as speaking the truth, which are rather clearly moral and not civil law examples.

---

[51] Psalm 15:2-3.

The moral law examples of not lending at interest are the baseline, elementary school-level examples of how we ought to behave in this regard, and Jesus actually chooses this as an example to expound on the true heart of the law behind the usury prohibition in Luke 6. "And if you lend to those from whom you expect repayment, what credit is that to you? Even sinners lend to sinners, expecting to be repaid in full. But love your enemies, do good to them, and lend to them without expecting to get anything back. Then your reward will be great, and you will be children of the Most High, because he is kind to the ungrateful and wicked" (Luke 6:34-35). Baseline (the Old Law) *justice* expectations are when you lend to someone expecting to receive back what you lent them. Baseline (the Old Law) *injustice* would be any time that you lent to someone expecting to receive back more than you loaned, which would be usury. And the New Covenant in the true spirit of the Law would expect a heart so generous that we would be willing to lend to others even in situations where we did not expect to get back what we lent.

In physics, you have the principle that for every action, there is an equal and opposite reaction. I find these laws of physics to also be quite instructive on the impacts of sin and love. Without grace, one sin would set off a never-ending chain reaction of increasing depravity that would not end until the whole world was consumed with evil. If someone wrongs me, the natural reaction is to wrong them back, and then they would want to retaliate again. Then I would want to retaliate, and so on, until we've killed each other or certainly fully severed our relationship. And I'm quite sure this self-destructive retaliatory instinct existed back in the beginning after our very first sin. "Eve! Why did you eat the fruit!? Now look at us and what you've done!" "Adam! You're really blaming *me* for this?! *You* told me not to even *touch* the fruit, but God didn't tell you that, He just said don't eat it. You must have ignored him like you ignore me all the time when I'm trying to tell you about my day. You're so selfish!"

It's a miracle that Adam and Eve loved each other enough after the fruit incident to start a family to populate the rest of the earth. And when I say it's a miracle that they could even start a family, I mean that quite literally. If we take C. S. Lewis's definition of a miracle "as an interference with Nature by supernatural power,"[52] you see this immediately after Adam and Eve's first sin and preceding Cain's

---

[52] C. S. Lewis, *Miracles* (New York: Harper Collins, 1974), 5.

conception. In God's grace, He clothes Adam and Eve in garments of skin, presumably shedding the blood of animals, establishing the principle that bloodshed is required for the atonement of sins (Genesis 3:21). When someone displays an act of love towards you, you often have an instinct to pay it forward. Love, which always begins from God, has its supernatural physics, an imposition from the supernatural into our physical world that sets off its chain reaction of increasing acts of love from the recipient of love towards others. God is love, and through the entirety of the Bible and in all of creation, you see His love for us, beginning with the first documented act of grace in Genesis 3:21 through Jesus Christ suffering a brutal and unjust death on our behalf. "This is how we know what love is: Jesus Christ laid down his life for us. And we ought to lay down our lives for our brothers and sisters" (1 John 3:16).

Now in this life, we have these warring avalanches of sin and love that we can usually quite easily see if we look out at the world or into our souls. You can usually find amazing acts of love and kindness in the world, but you can also quite easily find the most horrendous acts of depravity with a quick search online or by watching the first few minutes of a news program. I find the same principles at work in my soul - I now see some love there, prompted first by the grace of God, but I also see endless chasms of sin and self-interest that remain.

Since sin has entered the world, our default condition is to separate ourselves from God - "Once you were alienated from God and were enemies in your minds because of your evil behavior" (Colossians 1:21). We begin as enemies of God, but with God's grace, we can become aware of our hopeless situation before Him through the knowledge that there is such a thing as right and wrong and an awareness that none of us always does what is right. This awareness that we do wrong comes about through "the Law," which in this context would be equally true considering a broad range of meanings for the word law from the Torah, natural law, or any divine law examples. Praise be to God, though, that He loves us so much that He sent His only begotten son, Jesus Christ, as an atoning sacrifice for our sins. "But now he has reconciled you by Christ's physical body through death to present you holy in his sight, without blemish and free from accusation" (Colossians 1:22).

Being justified by God's grace and saved from the consequences of our sin is not the end of the story, though. God loves us too much to leave us with the horrid state of our sin, and if we are to be reconciled fully with Him eventually, knowing we can't take any of our sin with us, we might as well start earnestly seeking His grace to transform every wicked part of our soul into one properly fit towards acts of love. He will not stop until we are perfected, no matter how painful the love and pruning process may be. "Be perfect, therefore, as your heavenly Father is perfect" (Matthew 5:48).

We are sons and daughters, redeemed by the Father in love, and gifted with the Holy Spirit to guide us to serve in love and no longer cower in fear, but we are not to flaunt our status as an excuse to sin or ignore God's commands. "If you love me, keep my commands. And I will ask the Father, and he will give you another advocate to help you and be with you forever— the Spirit of truth. The world cannot accept him, because it neither sees him nor knows him. But you know him, for he lives with you and will be in you" (John 14:15-17).

God has made His commands around usury quite clear to us. If we claim to love God, we have no excuse not to obey them.

4. Tradition and Reason Against Usury

"If indeed someone has fallen into the error of presuming to affirm pertinaciously that the practice of usury is not sinful, we decree that he is to be punished as a heretic." - Council of Vienne (1311-1312 A.D.)[53]

Having reviewed the precarious nature of our economic environment at a macro level and the specific biblical texts relating to usury, I think we would now benefit from diving into the traditional Christian and philosophical arguments around usury. Using this as a framework will address some of the questions and objections that I suspect are still at the top of mind. By this time, I imagine a reader may be wondering about things such as whether interest should not be charged to cover the risk of non-repayment of a loan, whether the opportunity cost of a loan should not justify usury, or whether business loans should be treated the same as consumption loans, etc. We will get to these specific questions in short order. Still, since most of these questions are not new, but rather have been debated in some form or another for centuries, I think we would benefit first from placing them within the context of the philosophical and Christian tradition on this topic.

Suffice it to say that the position that usury is a sin and that usury is defined as receiving any amount greater than that which was loaned is not a radical or new belief. For almost 1,500 years, or nearly three-quarters of the Christian faith tradition, this belief was the nearly universally accepted position. The idea that usury was not a sin would have seemed as foreign as a justification that lying, theft, or murder was not sinful. It was just part and parcel of the Christian faith. One may say, "Well, yeah, we're just smarter now and know things they didn't know back then. Do you still think the Earth is flat and the Sun revolves around the Earth?" Well, no, I do not believe those things. However, I do not believe those things because our knowledge of the earth's position relative to the rest of the universe has improved alongside technological improvements that enable us to see these things better than our ancestors could. But are we that

---

[53] *Papal Encyclicals Online*, "Council of Vienne 1311-1312 A. D., *Papal Encyclicals Online*, https://www.papalencyclicals.net/councils/ecum15.htm

much smarter as it relates to money? What technological advancements or intellectual breakthroughs allow us to dissect money much better than our ancestors? C. S. Lewis described chronological snobbery as "the uncritical acceptance of the intellectual climate of our own age and the assumption that whatever has gone out of date is on that count discredited."[54] I can hardly imagine a more perfect application of this idea than with usury. It's thought to be ridiculous even to question the idea that usury is a sin. Still, those who scoff at the question can never point to some obvious monetary Copernican revolution or some eureka moment when it all became clear. We would be wise to follow Lewis's advice on the matter and understand "why did this idea go out of date? Was it ever refuted? If so, by whom, where, and how conclusively?"

Part 1: Early Church Against Usury

As it relates to the starting point that usury is a sin, you basically have a "who's who" of the most prominent early church fathers, all speaking unanimously on the matter. Here are a few quotes, as a non-exhaustive but illustrative list, mostly gleaned from the list of meticulously gathered sources in Michael Hoffman's book, *Usury in Christendom*:

Clement of Alexandria quotes Ezekiel in the *Paedagogus* in 198: "His money he will not give on usury, and will not take interest; and he will turn away his hand from wrong, and will execute righteous judgment between a man and his neighbour.'...'These words contain a description of the conduct of Christians, a notable exhortation to the blessed life, which is the reward of a life of goodness-- everlasting life.'"[55]

Tertullian again quotes Ezekiel in his treatise *Against Marcion* in 208: "And now, on the subject of a loan, when He asks, And if you lend to them of whom you hope to receive, what thank do you have? Compare with this the following words of Ezekiel, in which He says of the before-mentioned just man, He has not given his money upon usury, nor will he take any increase — meaning the

---

[54] C. S. Lewis, *Surprised by Joy: The Shape of My Early Life* (London: Harper Collins, 1955), 241.
[55] *Early Christian* Writings, Clement of Alexandria, *Paedagogus,* Chapter X, Book 1, http://www.earlychristianwritings.com/text/clement-instructor-book1.html

redundance of interest, which is usury."[56]

St. Cyprian of Carthage quotes the Psalms, Deuteronomy, and Ezekiel in *Ad Quirinum*: "In the thirteenth Psalm: He that has not given his money upon usury, and has not received gifts concerning the innocent. He who does these things shall not be moved forever. Also in Ezekiel: But the man who will be righteous, shall not oppress a man, and shall return the pledge of the debtor, and shall not commit rapine, and shall give his bread to the hungry, and shall cover the naked, and shall not give his money for usury. Also in Deuteronomy: You shall not lend to your brother with usury of money, and with usury of victuals."[57]

Michael Hoffman details how "St. Jerome in his *Commentaria in Ezechielem* stated that the prohibition against usury among the Israelites had been made universal by the New Testament. He affirmed that all interest on money is forbidden. 'One should never receive more than the amount loaned.'[58]

St. Basil (329 - 379) rails against usury in his homily on Psalm 15: "In depicting the character of the perfect man, of him, that is, who is ordained to ascend to the life of everlasting peace, the prophet reckons among his noble deeds his never having given his money upon usury. This particular sin is condemned in many passages of scripture. Ezekiel reckons taking usury and increase among the greatest of crimes. The law distinctly utters the prohibition 'Thou shalt not lend upon usury to thy brother' and to thy neighbor. Again it is said, 'Usury upon usury; guile upon guile.' And of the city abounding in a multitude of wickednesses, what does the Psalm say? 'Usury and guile depart not from her streets.' Now the prophet instances precisely the same point as characteristic of the perfect man, saying, 'He that putteth not out his money to usury.' For in truth it is the last pitch of inhumanity that one man, in need of the bare necessities of life, should be compelled to borrow, and another, not satisfied with the principal, should seek to make gain and profit for himself out of the calamities of the poor.[59]

---

[56] *New Advent*, Tertullian, *Against Marcion*, Chapter 17, Book 4, https://www.newadvent.org/fathers/03124.htm
[57] *New Advent*, St. Cyprian of Carthage, *Ad Quirinum*, Treatise 12, Third Book, chapter 48, https://www.newadvent.org/fathers/050712c.htm
[58] Michael Hoffman, *Usury in Christendom: The Mortal Sin that Was and Now Is Not* (New York: Independent History and Research, 2012), 67.
[59] *Early Church Texts*, Saint Basil, "The Great Homily on Psalm 14, Against Usury," https://earlychurchtexts.com/public/basil_homily_psalm_14_against_usury.htm

St. Gregory of Nyssa (circa 379 A.D.) details the following about usury: "Whoever receives money through usury takes a pledge of poverty and under the pretense of a good deed brings ruin on someone's home. You might perforce give wine out of charity to someone who is sick with a raging fever, if he is overcome with thirst and asks you for a drink. It brings him relief for a while when he takes the cup, but after a little while it makes his fever strong and ten times worse. In the same way if you give money laden with poverty to a poor man you are not relieving his distress but adding to his misfortune."[60]

St. Ambrose in De Tobia (380) writes: "Why, the very law of the Lord teaches us that this rule must be observed, so that we may never deprive another of anything for the sake of our own advantage...It forbids the laborer to be deprived of his hire, and orders money to be returned without usury. It is a mark of kindly feeling to help him who has nothing, *but it is a sign of a hard nature to extort more than one has given*. If a man has need of thy assistance because he has not enough of his own wherewith to repay a debt, *is it not a wicked thing to demand under the guise of kindly feeling a larger sum from him who has not the means to pay off a less amount?*[61]

St. John Crysostom (347 - 407) writes in Homily 5 on Matthew: "For nothing, nothing is baser than the usury of this world, nothing more cruel. Why, other persons' calamities are such a man's traffic; he makes himself gain of the distress of another, and demands wages for kindness, as though he were afraid to seem merciful, and under the cloak of kindness he digs the pitfall deeper, by the act of help galling a man's poverty, and in the act of stretching out the hand thrusting him down, and when receiving him as in harbor, involving him in shipwreck, as on a rock, or shoal, or reef."[62]

Pope St. Leo the Great writes in 444: "Neither do we think that it should be lightly passed over that some people, seized with the desire for filthy lucre, put out their money at usury in order to

[60] *Early Church Texts*, Gregory of Nyssa, "Oratio Contra Usurarios, https://earlychurchtexts.com/public/gregoryofnyss_contra_usurarios.htm
[61] *Internet Archive*, Phillip Schaff, *The Nicene and Post-Nicene Fathers of the Christian Church*, Saint Ambrose, "St. Ambrose: Selected Works and Letters," Chapter 3, section 20, https://archive.org/stream/St.AmbroseSelectedWorksAndLetters/st_ambrose_selected_works _and_letters_djvu.txt
[62] *New Advent*, Saint John Chrysostom, "Homily 5 on Matthew," Chapter 5, section 9, https://www.newadvent.org/fathers/200105.htm

become rich thereby. And we have to complain of this not only with regard to those in clerical office but we likewise grieve to see that it holds true of lay people who wish to be called Christians. We decree that this should be severely punished in those found guilty, so that all occasion of sin may be washed away."[63]

St. Austine writes in *Expositions on the Psalms* in the early 5th century: "If thou hast lent thy money on usury to man, that is, if thou hast given the loan of thy money to one, from whom thou dost expect to receive something more than thou hast given, not in money only, but any thing, whether it be wheat, or wine, or oil, or whatever else you please, if you expect to receive more than you have given, you are an usurer, and in this particular are not deserving of praise, but of censure."[64]

Several church councils have also spoken directly on the matter of usury:

In the Council of Nicea in 325 in Canon 17, you have the following: "Forasmuch as many enrolled among the Clergy, following covetousness and lust of gain, have forgotten the divine Scripture, which says, *He has not given his money upon usury,* and in lending money ask the hundredth of the sum, the holy and great Synod thinks it just that if after this decree any one be found to receive usury, whether he accomplish it by secret transaction or otherwise, as by demanding the whole and one half, or by using any other contrivance whatever for filthy lucre's sake, he shall be deposed from the clergy and his name stricken from the list."[65]

In the Third Lateran Council of 1179 in Canon 25, you have the following: "Nearly everywhere the crime of usury has become so firmly rooted that many, omitting other business, practice usury as if it were permitted, and in no way observe how it is forbidden in both the Old and New Testament. We therefore declare that notorious usurers should not be admitted to communion of the altar or receive christian burial if they die in this sin. Whoever receives them or gives them christian burial should be compelled to give back what

---

[63] J. P. Migne, ed. *Patrologiae Cursus Completus*, (Paris: 1845), Vols. XXV, p. 177, CLXXXVII, 959, reprinted in Roy C. Cave & Herbert H. Coulson, *A Source Book for Medieval Economic History,* (Milwaukee: The Bruce Publishing Co., 1936; reprint ed., New York: Biblo & Tannen, 1965), 170-171.

[64] *New Advent*, Saint Augustine, *Expositions on the Psalms*, "Exposition on Psalm 37," https://www.newadvent.org/fathers/1801037.htm

[65] *New Advent*, "First Council of Nicaea," https://www.newadvent.org/fathers/3801.htm

he has received, and let him remain suspended from the performance of his office until he has made satisfaction according to the judgment of his own bishop."[66]

In the Second Council of Lyons in 1274, you have the following: "Wishing to close up the abyss of usury, which devours souls and swallows up property, we order under threat of the divine malediction that the constitution of the Lateran council against usurers be inviolably observed. Since the less convenient it is for usurers to lend, the more their freedom to practice usury is curtailed, we ordain by this general constitution as follows. Neither a college, nor other community, nor an individual person, of whatever dignity, condition or status, may permit those foreigners and others not originating from their territories, who practice usury or wish to do so, to rent houses for that purpose or to occupy rented houses or to live elsewhere. Rather, they must expel all such notorious usurers from their territories within three months, never to admit any such for the future."[67]

At the council of Vienne in 1311, you have the following: "Serious suggestions have been made to us that communities in certain places, to the divine displeasure and injury of the neighbor, in violation of both divine and human law, approve of usury. By their statutes, sometimes confirmed by oath, they not only grant that usury may be demanded and paid, but deliberately compel debtors to pay it. By these statutes they impose heavy burdens on those claiming the return of usurious payments, employing also various pretexts and ingenious frauds to hinder the return. We, therefore, wishing to get rid of these pernicious practices, decree with the approval of the sacred council that all the magistrates, captains, rulers, consuls, judges, counsellors or any other officials of these communities who presume in the future to make, write or dictate such statutes, or knowingly decide that usury be paid or, if paid, that it be not fully and freely restored when claimed, incur the sentence of excommunication. They shall also incur the same sentence unless within three months they delete from the books of their communities, if they have the power, statutes of this kind hitherto published, or if they presume to observe in any way these statutes or customs. Furthermore, since money-lenders for the most part

[66] *Papal Encyclicals Online,* "Third Lateran Council- 1779 A. D.," https://www.papalencyclicals.net/councils/ecum11.htm
[67] *Papal Encyclicals Online*, "Second Council of Lyons- 1274," https://www.papalencyclicals.net/councils/ecum14.htm

enter into usurious contracts so frequently with secrecy and guile that they can be convicted only with difficulty, we decree that they be compelled by ecclesiastical censure to open their account books, when there is question of usury. If indeed someone has fallen Into the error of presuming to affirm pertinaciously that the practice of usury is not sinful, we decree that he is to be punished as a heretic; and we strictly enjoin on local ordinaries and inquisitors of heresy to proceed against those they find suspect of such error as they would against those suspected of heresy.[68]

The above does not even include other examples such as Charlemagne in 789 AD that "prohibited usury by all people, laymen as well as clerics, throughout the lands of the Holy Roman Empire," King Alfred the Great (849-899), that "ordered that the charging of interest on loans of money was illegal throughout England,"[69] or numerous other influential writers, theologians, and Popes that condemned usury such as Pope Urban III, Pope Alexander III, St. Anselm (1033-1109), St. Albert the Great (1193-1280), St. Bonaventure (1221-1274), and Dante Alighieri.[70] I will pause with the detailed quotes as I suspect you get the picture by now.

Throughout these examples, you have repeated condemnations of usury, and while many of the instances simply assume the definition of usury, in those where usury is defined, it refers to *any* increase in principal (e.g., St. Ambrose - *to extort more than one has given,* St. Augustine - *if thou hast given the loan of thy money to one from whom thou dost expect to receive something more than thou hast given).*

Part 2: Faith, Reason, and Usury

In most of the examples discussed thus far, and throughout around the first thousand or so years of the church, the condemnations of usury typically did not coincide with a natural law argument explaining why usury was a sin beyond explaining how it violated divine law, but with the rise of Scholasticism around the 11th and 12th centuries, you have what Noonan describes as "an immense interest in showing the rational basis for the duty commanded by God." "The scholastics do not depend on authority or revelation or

[68] *Papal Encyclicals Online*, "Council of Vienne- 1311-1312 A. D.,"
https://www.papalencyclicals.net/councils/ecum15.htm
[69] Hoffman, *Usury in Christendom*, 72.
[70] Hoffman, *Usury in Christendom*, 74-77.

Roman law alone. Increasingly, they make a determined effort to rest their case against usury on the nature of man and on the nature of things in themselves; similarly they try to determine what forms of credit are naturally lawful and just. Attempting to appeal to reason alone, they build the structure of the usury theory."[71]

In short order, I think we will benefit from investigating the view on usury from the Scholastic perspective as the typical responses we moderns provide when discussing the morality of usury are often quite like the debates from the Scholastic period. Many, if not most, in the Western world today proudly think of ourselves as being ruled by reason, or our ability to think, understand, and form judgments by logic. And this is not bad - praise God for the gift of reason. And yet, before we dive into the natural law and reasoned debates for and against usury, I would first like to begin with a few points to consider as there are pitfalls to be wary of in our sometimes hubristic exaltation in our ability to reason. Firstly, we must never forget that our reason is dependent upon faith, or as Peter Kreeft puts it in expounding on Pascal, "To reason is to rely on reason, and to rely on reason is an act of faith, not of reason. Therefore reason presupposes faith."[72] Without the assumption that we have been gifted with minds that can ascertain truth and that truth is even real, there can be no such thing as reason. Reason cannot prove reason - reason sits on the shoulders of faith, and faith extends beyond reason, so please never forget which both came first and will remain last ("And now these three remain: faith, hope and love"[73]).

But beyond simply appreciating the origin of reason, we must also keep in mind that our reason is not infallible - our syllogisms and deductions are not always flawless, even in the hands of those with the purest of hearts. But perhaps even greater consideration should be given to the risk that we are not being ruled by reason, even when we think we are, but rather by our passions, especially as it relates to considerations around usury that may implicate our most cherished god - money. When we reason about usury, are we sincerely seeking truth on the matter, or are we reasoning *from* already decided presuppositions about the morality of lending at interest to defend a position that we desire to be true?

---

[71] John T. Noonan, Jr., *The Scholastic Analysis of Usury* (London: Oxford University Press, 1957), 3.
[72] Kreeft, *Christianity for Modern Pagans*, 110.
[73] 1 Corinthians 13:13.

In *The Happiness Hypothesis* by Jonathan Haidt, Haidt uses the metaphor of the rider and the elephant to describe the relation between our passions and our reason as he says: "Modern theories about rational choice and information processing don't adequately explain weakness of the will. The older metaphors about controlling animals work beautifully. The image that I came up with for myself, as I marveled at my weakness, was that I was a rider on the back of an elephant. I'm holding the reins in my hands, and by pulling one way or the other I can tell the elephant to turn, to stop, or to go. I can direct things, but only when the elephant doesn't have desires of his own. When the elephant really wants to do something, I'm no match for him."[74] In this example, the elephant reflects our emotions, passions, or unreflective desires, whereas the rider on the back of the elephant represents our thoughtful reasoning capacities. While we like to think that our reason drives the elephant, even a resolute rider will be hapless to redirect an elephant who is staunchly committed to another path. Such is how it goes with our reason - our reason is helpless to redirect passions and desires run amok in another direction. Haidt is in good company with metaphors such as the rider and the elephant as it resembles Plato's charioteer (as Haidt points out himself) where the charioteer (reason) controls two horses, with one horse especially prone to appetitive lusts, which can make it nearly impossible for reason to control when the horse runs off after its passions. And of course, you have St. Paul in scripture alluding to a similar phenomenon where we find ourselves unable to do the things that part of us desires to do, such as in the following example in Romans - "For I know that nothing good dwells in me, that is, in my flesh. For I have the desire to do what is right, but not the ability to carry it out."[75]

I suspect anyone who honestly reflects on bad things they have done will find these metaphors to reveal much truth. When we do unquestionably wrong things by even our standards of value, our initial reaction will often be to grasp for some *reason* to justify our behavior. While our passions lead us to our destination, our reason convinces us that it's driving the bus and makes up a plausible explanation for how we got there.

I bring up these points about our passions driving our reason because regardless of whether the change in moral sentiments on a

---

[74] Jonathan Haidt, *The Happiness Hypothesis: Finding Modern Truth in Ancient Wisdom* (New York: Basic Books, 2006), 4.
[75] Romans 7:18.

matter such as usury was due to soberly thoughtful or passionately spurious reasoning, there will not appear to be a difference between these two situations at first glance, as those in both situations will appeal to reason. Therefore, we should be careful just to assume that reason carried the day when explaining significant moral changes, and we should be especially critical when thinking through the stated reasons for such a large shift in morality in something such as usury where a passion for profit without work could be lurking beneath the surface of our explanations.

Although not directly tying the reasons to our passions as referenced above, Noonan makes an interesting statement in the introduction to his fabulously thorough investigation into the Scholastic views of usury regarding how presuppositions can inform one's views on usury when he writes the following, "Undeniably, the scholastics are all either theologians or canonists; undeniably they start their investigation with an awareness of the teaching of the Church; and undeniably their opinions will not run counter to her positive determinations."[76] The piece of Noonan's statement that I find interesting is how he seems quick to assert, perhaps justifiably, that presuppositions of those in the early scholastic period could have already been decided against usury, before the rational investigation of its morality, as these views were established by the church. Yet, he does not seem to consider how the same temptation could easily exist on the other foot in those that eventually reasoned away most of the convictions against usury as he says that "the later scholastics did correct their predecessors' zeal; and it is in the medieval period itself that the theory of legitimate interest and alternative methods of credit originates."[77] It seems quite arbitrary to me to assert this principle on one side of the argument while ignoring the likelihood on the other. Are those bringing forth reasons for exception after exception relating to why the usury condemnation should be softened, not equally subject to zealous presuppositions by desires for profit or the growing appeals to the pragmatism of commerce in the later scholastic period? It seems as if Augustine would affirm the scholastics expounding the reasons against usury even if prompted by the origins of the holy Scriptures. "Thus, since we are too weak by unaided reason to find out the truth, and since, because of this, we need the authority of the holy writings, I had now begun to believe that thou wouldst not, under any

---

[76] Noonan, *Scholastic Analysis of Usury*, 3.
[77] Noonan, *Scholastic Analysis of Usury*, 4.

circumstances, have given such eminent authority to those Scriptures throughout all lands if it had not been that through them thy will may be believed in and that thou might be sought."[78] One's heart may affirm the truth gleaned from the Church or scripture and then reason how this makes sense, while another's heart may affirm the prevailing economic theories of the day and then reason how their predetermined position makes sense. Still, the temptation to let reason be driven by our passion infused presuppositions certainly exists in both circumstances.

It's quite an interesting conundrum we're in - we're left to grasp for the truth through our use of reason, and all the while, our reason could be nothing more than a tool to justify a position already presupposed by the depths of our heart's innermost desires. As Pascal so wisely put it, "The heart has its reasons, of which reason does not know."[79] So, regardless of our side in the usury debate, I suspect our outward reflections and dialogues in the name of reason could be nothing more than a manifestation of our faith in either God or money. Yet, I still believe exercising our reason is immensely beneficial. While the mechanics of conversion, whether in a repentant turn towards God or even in just a substantial change in perspective on any number of issues, continues to bewilder me, reason seems to either open a crack into the chasms of our heart such that it prepares ourselves to be transformed by the Light, or it offers an opportunity for us to strengthen the muscles of our faith gifted to us by God. I believe the maxim often attributed to Augustine, "Understanding is the reward of faith. Therefore seek not to understand that you may believe, but believe that you may understand." And yet, in Augustine you have someone who paradoxically both reasons better than most in the history of the known world, and yet also readily admits the limits of reason. While it may remain somewhat mysterious whether proper reasoning is simply the effect of faith gifted to us by God or whether striving towards proper reasoning and discernment of truth serves as a cause of faith, we ought to seek out understanding as best as we can with prayers of petition for faith and acts of reason to understand.

Additionally, while reason has its limitations, and I believe Noonan has overstated the quality and rigor of the reasoning that essentially neutered the previous convictions against usury, I do agree with his

---

[78] Augustine, *Confessions*, 6:5.
[79] Pascal, *Pensees* (New York: E. P. Dutton and Co., Inc., 1958), 277.

position that an understanding of the principles in matters of morals is often necessary if we are to have any hope to apply these to our daily lives. "Moral rules do not exist in a vacuum: they must be applied; and to apply a rule to human conduct means first that its rational foundation and purpose must be discovered in order that the type of acts it prescribes or prohibits may successfully be determined. At the same time it means that distinctions between different related acts will be found, exceptions recognized, logical extensions made, and deductions drawn. This is the task of human reason, and it is indispensable to the life of morals."[80] So, while reason has its challenges, its use cannot, nor should not be avoided, in discerning matters of morals. Therefore, we will scan the history of the reasoned analysis around the morality of usury, diving into where it is fruitful to do so and praying that the Lord will guide our thoughts along the way. I pray that the use of reason may be a useful vessel to reveal truth to those in error and offer a pathway for the Lord to turn our hearts toward truth.

There remains one last challenge that must be acknowledged from the outset before expounding on the reasons for and against usury, and that relates to the fact that most of us reason for our moral decisions from different frameworks or foundations. Some will focus on our duty, ignoring speculation on the expected outcome, while others will focus almost exclusively on anticipating the outcomes of our actions. Some emphasize the objective nature of morals and seek to find the application of universal principles in specific situations. In contrast, others cite the variance of attitudes in morality as proof there is no objective standard at all and, therefore, claim that assessments of right and wrong reside in the eye of the beholder. Some believe the ultimate objective of life is happiness, with the idea of happiness closely resembling a nature molded in virtue resilient to external circumstances. In contrast, others believe the ultimate objective of life is to seek happiness by achieving pleasurable goals and avoiding painful circumstances. Some proudly emphasize self over others and encourage loved ones to "do what's best for you," while others emphasize the other and encourage you to "put yourself in the other's shoes." Achieving comprehensiveness in analyzing the reasons for and against usury from *all* these different perspectives would be almost impossible. As I wrote at the outset, I hope to convince you that usury is wrong, and usury is receiving any amount greater than you loaned. Therefore, I will focus on the reasons that I believe will be most persuasive to

---

[80] Noonan, *Scholastic Analysis of Usury*, 3.

those reading this book, which will include considerations from several of these frameworks throughout the discussion, without a goal of comprehensiveness.

Part 3: Reasoned Arguments Against Usury

With those caveats out of the way, I think the best place to start understanding the arguments against usury from reason is with Aristotle, who denounced usury in *Politics* in the 4th century BC. While the arguments from Aristotle may sound foreign to our modern ears as they are rooted in natural law arguments, which are not as common today, his position is a great primer to begin to understand some of the other prominent arguments against usury based on natural law foundations. While certainly an oversimplification, natural law arguments can typically be rooted in the purposes of things. Properly aligning towards the ends or purposes of things results in good, and going against the ends or purposes results in evil. As Aquinas puts it, "Good has the nature of an end, and evil, the nature of a contrary, hence it is that all those things to which man has a natural inclination, are naturally apprehended by reason as being good, and consequently as objects of pursuit, and their contraries as evil, and objects of avoidance."[81] Now please do not misconstrue this quote to think that Aquinas means that whatever we desire at all times is good, as he later elaborates how our reason can be corrupted and cause us to fail in adhering to natural laws - "But as to certain matters of detail, which are conclusions, as it were, of those general principles...in some few cases it may fail, both as to rectitude, by reason of certain obstacles (just as natures subject to generation and corruption fail in some few cases on account of some obstacle), and as to knowledge, since in some the reason is perverted by passion, or evil habit, or an evil disposition of nature"[82]

While Aquinas is writing around 1500 years after Aristotle as he explains natural law, these same ideas hold when understanding the perspective Aristotle had around usury when he writes the following:

"There are two sorts of wealth-getting, as I have said; one is a part of household management, the other is retail trade: the former

---

[81] Aquinas, *Summa Theologica*, First Part of the Second Part, Question 94, Article 2.
[82] Aquinas, *Summa Theologica*, First Part of the Second Part, Question 94, Article 4.

necessary and honorable, while that which consists in exchange is justly censured; for it is unnatural, and a mode by which men gain from one another. The most hated sort, and with the greatest reason, is usury, which makes a gain out of money itself, and not from the natural object of it. For money was intended to be used in exchange, but not to increase at interest. And this term interest, which means the birth of money from money, is applied to the breeding of money because the offspring resembles the parent. Wherefore of any modes of getting wealth this is the most unnatural."[83]

If you are seeing this quote for the first time, I would caution you not to dismiss this too quickly out of hand based on his comment about retail trade. The origin of our word "economy" is from the Greek term, *oikonomia*, which refers to the concept of household management, basically referring to being able to produce or procure the amount and types of goods that are necessary for a household to thrive. So when Aristotle praises wealth getting as part of household management but condemns it as part of retail trade, I believe he primarily has in mind that wealth getting as part of household management refers to obtaining wealth for the particular purpose of supporting a household unit (whether that be a family or a larger societal entity), whereas obtaining wealth as part of retail trade is condemned as this activity then would have been associated with seeking wealth simply for the sake of wealth. Money should be treated as a means to a greater end but never as an end itself. When one does not eat, they become hungry and have an appropriate desire for food, which can be met after this person eats food. The desire for hunger does not extend to infinity. So, seeking money for the sake of procuring food is a fine motive because it can be used as an intermediary for an appropriate end; however, pursuing money for the sake of money has no limit. If one desires money for the sake of money, this desire is not quenched upon acquiring money, as this is not a natural desire. How much money will make someone happy, you may ask? More.

In the chapter before his quote about usury, Aristotle speaks to this point when he says: "Like in the fable, who from his insatiable wish had everything he touched turned into gold. For which reason others endeavour to procure other riches and other property, and rightly, for there are other riches and property in nature; and these are the proper objects of economy: while trade only procures

---

[83] Aristotle, *Politics*, Chapter 10.

money, not by all means, but by the exchange of it, and for that purpose it is this which it is chiefly employed about, for money is the first principle and the end of trade; nor are there any bounds to be set to what is thereby acquired…for economy requires the possession of wealth, but not on its own account but with another view, to purchase things necessary therewith; but the other procures it merely to increase it: so that some persons are confirmed in their belief, that this is the proper object of economy, and think that for this purpose money should be saved and hoarded up without end."[84]

While I think the value of retail trade relating to logistics and planning to prepare goods such that they can be acquired by others may be unfairly diminished in this example from Aristotle, I think we would be wise to take heed of his caution around seeking money for money's sake, which I believe is the main point he is getting at. And while this part of the quote is not entirely germane to my argument about usury, I hope this explanation will soften some knee-jerk reactions to dismiss the entirety of Aristotle's point outright as the ramblings from some ancient fool.

Now as Aristotle continues beyond condemning the pursuit of money for the sake of money itself, he enters his argument about usury, which is similar to the previous argument about the unnaturalness of this method of wealth acquisition, except with usury he speaks to how much *more* unnatural this type of wealth acquisition is than retail trade intended purely for the sake of profit. To restate his point again, "The most hated sort, and with the greatest reason, is usury, which makes a gain out of money itself, and not from the natural object of it. For money was intended to be used in exchange, but not to increase at interest. And this term interest, which means the birth of money from money, is applied to the breeding of money because the offspring resembles the parent. Wherefore of any modes of getting wealth this is the most unnatural."[85] Whereas retail trade at least uses money for its proper end (exchange), it uses money in line with its proper end to achieve unnatural ends at a higher level (the pursuit of money for money's sake). However, with usury, you have a double whammy because this type of activity not only runs the risk of pursuing money for money's sake, but you are perverting the nature of money because

---

[84] Aristotle, *Politics*, Part 9.
[85] Aristotle, *Politics*, Book 1, Part 10, https://classics.mit.edu/Aristotle/politics.1.one.html

money was intended to be exchanged, not to give birth to more money. Said another way, you are unnaturally using money to achieve unnatural ends. You are using money unnaturally (by seeking for it to give birth to more money), and you are using it to achieve an unnatural desire (the pursuit of profit for the sake of profit).

Suffice it to say that you do not find many people today debating either for or against the merits of Aristotle's arguments against usury, as the topic of usury is typically just dismissed entirely. However, in the few instances where you can still find serious intellectual engagement on the issue of usury, I am surprised at how quickly the Aristotelian claim seems to be dismissed. As just one example, one of the greatest minds I have found on the usury topic thus far, S. C. Mooney, dismisses Aristotle's argument without further elaboration, saying, "It is not much of a case." While Mooney's intellect and analysis on this issue seem to dwarf mine in so many ways, I still cautiously find the Aristotelian argument against usury quite compelling, as all the critiques I have found against it seem lacking.[86]

The strongest critiques I could imagine one would have against Aristotle's argument would be to say that there is no difference in how money can grow into more money and how seeds can grow into crops. While I have never heard these types of claims framed as a specific rebuttal against Aristotle, I commonly hear statements such as these discussed in different financial or business conversations in a more general sense. No one debates that seeds can grow into plants, and this growth is wonderful, yet seeds do not just magically grow into crops to be harvested. While plants can grow under conditions without any human intervention, they typically flourish the most under thoughtful planning and labor to create the conditions such that the potential of seeds can be best fulfilled by them growing into plants that can be harvested for food. So, it's not just seeds birthing plants, but seeds *and labor* birthing more plants. Is it not the same for money? Money alone does not magically turn into more money, but money can be transformed into goods that can then be utilized to produce profit and more money. The problem with these statements is that when seeds transform into crops harvested into food, the final cause (or the purpose of the seeds) is to do just what happens - to become plants. However, the final cause (the purpose of money) is not to beget more money - the

---

[86] Mooney, *Usury: Destroyer of Nations*, 33.

purpose of money is to be exchanged. If money is exchanged for labor or material and after this initial exchange, that labor or those materials are utilized such that they create a greater product that is sold for more than the money that was initially exchanged (a profit), this is not primarily the cause of the money that leads to this. One could just as easily say that a seed grows cows as money grows money, and those statements are both true in one sense and absurd in another. A seed could grow into plants, and plants could grow into food, and the food could be traded for cows, such that the use of the seed results in the acquisition of the cow, but it's absurd to think that the seed grows cows on its own merit. The same is the case with money. The money can be traded for a lawnmower and human labor, and the lawnmower could be used to mow lawns and earn more money than was initially used to buy the lawnmower, but it's absurd to think the money does this on its own merit to grow more money. While labor and human thought are often one of the efficient causes that lead to the growth of seed into crops, in these situations the seed is fulfilling its final cause (the purpose of the seed is to become a plant) and the human inputs are just one of the efficient causes that leads to this result (alongside the complex biological processes that result in the growth of plants from seeds). However, in the instance of money, as money is exchanged for other items and those items are used to produce greater items that are then traded for more money, money does not continue to reach its final cause (its purpose) throughout this process. When money is exchanged for the labor or products that are ultimately used to generate a profit, money has already fulfilled its final cause when it was exchanged, as money exists to be exchanged. The effects after money is exchanged are not caused by the money, but by the things money was exchanged for. So, when Aristotle says, "For money was intended to be used in exchange, but not to increase at interest."[87] I still think he's right in this critique against usury.

Now while I do think the Aristotelian argument is underrated and I think it still has its merits today, I am not necessarily expecting that to be the one that wins many people over as it is rather complex, and we moderns are often not persuaded by natural law arguments such as this one. However, I think the Aristotelian argument offers a nice segue into the next reasoned argument worthy of detailed attention from Thomas Aquinas. When Aquinas comes onto the scene in the 13th century, you have had Christian tradition almost

---

[87] Aristotle, *Politics*, Book 1, Chapter 1, https://classics.mit.edu/Aristotle/politics.1.one.html

unanimously against usury for centuries (as explained at the outset of this chapter). While you are starting to see the arguments against usury extend beyond references to divine law alone and into arguments from reason, these are often still in their infancy stages and are somewhat scattered in how they are presented. With Aquinas, you have the clarity and comprehensive considerations that typically come from this intellectual powerhouse, and you also have claims that usury is a sin against justice and the delineation between usury and rent. I'll quote this example from Aquinas in length to start, and then we can drill into the high points:

"To take usury for money lent is unjust in itself, because this is to sell what does not exist, and this evidently leads to inequality which is contrary to justice. In order to make this evident, we must observe that there are certain things the use of which consists in their consumption: thus we consume wine when we use it for drink and we consume wheat when we use it for food. Wherefore in such like things the use of the thing must not be reckoned apart from the thing itself, and whoever is granted the use of the thing, is granted the thing itself and for this reason, to lend things of this kind is to transfer the ownership. Accordingly if a man wanted to sell wine separately from the use of the wine, he would be selling the same thing twice, or he would be selling what does not exist, wherefore he would evidently commit a sin of injustice. In like manner he commits an injustice who lends wine or wheat, and asks for double payment, viz. one, the return of the thing in equal measure, the other, the price of the use, which is called usury.

On the other hand, there are things the use of which does not consist in their consumption: thus to use a house is to dwell in it, not to destroy it. Wherefore in such things both may be granted: for instance, one man may hand over to another the ownership of his house while reserving to himself the use of it for a time, or vice versa, he may grant the use of the house, while retaining the ownership. For this reason a man may lawfully make a charge for the use of his house, and, besides this, revendicate the house from the person to whom he has granted its use, as happens in renting and letting a house.

Now money, according to the Philosopher was invented chiefly for the purpose of exchange: and consequently the proper and principal use of money is its consumption or alienation whereby it is sunk in exchange. Hence it is by its very nature unlawful to take payment for the use of money lent, which payment is known as usury: and just as a man is bound to restore other ill-gotten goods, so is he bound to restore the money which he has taken in usury."[88]

While I think Aquinas's explanation could probably just stand on its own without additional commentary, I will expound on this argument to the best of my own understanding in case this proves to be beneficial to the reader. In Roman law, there were different types of exchange contracts depending on 1) whether the contract was one of use or consumption and 2) whether or not there was a charge associated with the contract. As detailed by Noonan, "The Roman law had known two parallel gratuitous contracts and two parallel onerous contracts: the *commodatum* by which a good was freely transferred as to its use, and the *mutuum* by which a good was freely and temporarily transferred as to its ownership; the *locatio*, in which the commodatum was replaced by a charge for the use, and the *foenus*, in which by an added, positive stipulation a premium was charged for the loan."[89] While Aquinas was not the first to make these distinctions and use them in an argument against usury, he synthesized the thought from earlier theologians such as Robert of Courcon around these topics in a cogent manner.[90]

In the first paragraph of Aquinas's summary on usury, he speaks to loans of mutuum. He describes how money and things such as wheat or wine have two key characteristics: 1) their ownership is transferred upon exchange, and 2) they are consumed through their use. Therefore, in an exchange such as a loan of $100, whereby the lender provides the borrower $100 with the expectation that the borrower will return an equivalent amount of $100 to the lender at some agreed-upon time in the future, the ownership of the $100 effectively changes hands from the lender to the borrower at the time of the initial transfer of funds. It is not as if the lender expects to receive the exact same one-hundred-dollar bill back from the borrower or has any claim over the use of that particular $100 after it has been loaned (assuming there were no other separate terms in the contract that dictated the usage of the loan). Still, rather the lender just expects to receive an equivalent amount of this fungible currency back. The lender *uses* the $100 when he lends it to the borrower and currently transfers ownership of that $100 to the

---

[88] *New Advent*, Aquinas, *Summa Theologiae,* Second Part of the Second Part, Question 78, Article 1, https://www.newadvent.org/summa/3078.htm

[89] Noonan, *Scholastic Analysis of Usury*, 40.

[90] Noonan, *Scholastic Analysis of Usury*, 41.

borrower. So, according to Aquinas, in a loan of something such as money, you would be committing an injustice if you ask both for a) the return of the $100 and b) a charge to use the $100. As it relates to the $100 itself, it's an evident law of math that 1=1 and 100=100, so when someone lends $100 to someone, it's an injustice to expect more than $100 in and of itself as $100 = $100. There are no grounds to justify asking for more money if the entirety of the exchange is to lend $100 and receive back the same amount. And as it relates to the often-claimed second part of the transaction that you are charging for the "use" of money, this is charging for something that does not exist because as the lender you have relinquished your ownership rights of the $100 itself as the money is loaned, so you cannot claim also to be charging for the use of the $100, as that is something you don't have claim to.

In the second paragraph of Aquinas's summary on usury, he contrasts the loans of mutuum, whereby ownership is transferred alongside the use of the item, to the loans of commodatum whereby someone could reasonably transfer the use of an item while they still maintain the ownership of the item. This intuitively makes sense if you think about it. Suppose an owner of a house lets someone use it for a year at a cost (the owner rents the house). In that case, it's not as if the owner of the house just expects to receive the right to use "house" back at the end of the year in the sense of any generic house at any possible location, but rather the owner expects to receive back the rights to use the same house that he rented. If I rent a 3-bedroom, 2-bath house at 123 Main Street to someone, I expect the same 3-bedroom, 2-bath house at 123 Main Street at the end of the agreement, not just any house of any size or location. So, in this situation, it is reasonable to consider that the owner of the house still *owns* 123 Main Street even while it is in *use* by a different person, as the owner would remain accountable for certain aspects of the asset during its use by another person, the owner would still expect to receive back that same asset (and not just an equal kind and amount) at the end of the agreement, and the owner still retains risk of deterioration of the asset during the use of the asset by a different person.

At this point, we could take a long detour to debate the intricacies of whether rent should be considered usury as much more could be said and debated about what constitutes ownership and how that relates to rent and usury; however, I am not convinced I have the legal and philosophical depth to do this topic justice, and I do not believe the outcome would materially change the main points I am trying to make. In the medieval era and before in Christian societies, the foundational precedent was that usury was sinful and lending money (among other items) for profit was usury. Therefore, questions around the rent of goods such as houses and horses were to determine if these types of transactions were analogous enough to loans of money also to be considered usury, or whether they were different enough from what was already established as usury to be considered something different and licit. Said another way, money loans at profit were usury, and if rent was like money loans, then it would be concluded that rent was also usury. However, if rent was considered materially different from money loans, then it would not be considered usury. However, in modern times what I have found from experience on these topics is that individuals will often unreflectively start with the premise that renting goods such as a house is licit, and then hastily draw the comparison that renting houses is like renting money without providing reasons for their conclusion in this comparison, and therefore ultimately conclude that lending money at profit is licit and not usury. Said another way, we now often say rent is not sinful or usurious, and rent is like lending money at profit, and therefore lending money at profit is not sinful or usurious. To me, this is the wrong way to approach this question as we should start from the foundation that lending money at a profit is usury and sinful as this foundation has been established regardless of whether we approach this from a Biblical perspective, a church tradition perspective, or from a philosophical perspective. This foundation that lending money at profit is usury should be compared to whether rent should be included in this same lending category. I think the Roman law distinction and the distinction detailed by Aquinas make sense - lending money, wheat, or other commodity-type fungible items and expecting greater amounts in return is usury.[91] I consider the rent of goods such as a house or a car to be a different transaction that does not explicitly relate to usury. Whether these transactions should be considered sinful on entirely different merits could be debated. Still, I do not think they are usury, and considerations outside of usury are beyond the scope of this writing. However, even if someone were to convince me that renting a house is similar

---

[91] While the Biblical examples do leave open consideration to "anything else that could earn interest" in the examples of Deuteronomy and Leviticus, they only mention money and food specifically, and both of these fit within the categories as detailed by Aquinas and Roman law as transactions of mutuum, such that it seems most plausible to me that the "any other items" considered here would also follow along these same types of mutuum transactions as opposed to the commodatum types.

enough to lending money at a profit such that they should be treated the same way as it relates to usury considerations, this would just convince me that renting houses and other transactions such as this are *also* usury, it would not convince me that lending money at a profit is no longer usury.

Finally, in Aquinas's third paragraph, he summarizes the Aristotelian objection to usury, namely that using money for this purpose contradicts the nature of money. This portion stands well without further elaboration, especially considering we have already discussed Aristotle's main points earlier.

Of the three positions against usury that Noonan summarizes were primarily favored during the Scholastic period, we have already referenced the "Thomistic argument that the use and ownership of consumables are one" and the "argument that money bears no fruit."[92] Therefore, we will now turn to the final of the three most prominent arguments from this time- "the Andrean argument that fungibles have a fixed value."[93] Noonan summarizes the Andrean argument with the following: "things fixed in number, weight, or measure have an intrinsic value set upon them by their determined quantity; when the lender of such goods expects to receive a greater quantity than he gave, he attempts to make his goods 'worth more than their nature'; consequently, he acts unjustly and unnaturally."[94] This argument is probably the easiest to follow and is the same point as explained above in the explanation of the Thomistic argument. $100 by its very nature is worth $100. $100 cannot be worth $200. To ask for more back than the $100 that was loaned is to be making $100 worth more than it is worth and contrary to its nature, and therefore this is unjust.

Part 4: Piquing of Interest

While I find the Andrean argument to be compelling on its own merit, I find this argument to be especially beneficial to use as a launching point to understand both where the historical arguments around usury went next, and to use as a foundation to analyze the most common modern objections against considering usury a sin. Most people today would not dispute the Andrean argument by saying that $100 equals $110. Still, rather, they would say that when

---

[92] Noonan, *Scholastic Analysis of Usury*, 81.
[93] Noonan, *Scholastic Analysis of Usury*, 81.
[94] Noonan, *Scholastic Analysis of Usury*, 67.

you lend money at interest, you are not only justified in receiving $100, but you are justified in receiving the additional $10 for some other reason. It's not that $100 = $110, but rather $100 +$10 = $110, whereas the $10 should be due as compensation for some consideration *extrinsic* to the basic agreement of the loan. Whether it be because of claimed damages incurred by the lender, the opportunity cost of what the lender gives up when making the loan, the risk the lender takes when making the loan, or several other reasons, it could be argued that the lender should be compensated for something that on its own merit would be worthy of compensation. This line of debate was exactly the route of the historical treatment of usury, and it's probably the easiest way to understand the semantic shift in using "interest" and "usury" today. As noted by S.C. Mooney, "the medieval English term usury derived from the Larin *usuria*, and carried the more theoretical idea of selling the use of property,"[95] whereas what is now known as "interest" comes from the Latin *interess*, which means a compensatory payment. Towards the beginning stages of the usury debates where *extrinsic titles* were introduced, the term usury was still considered when any amount greater than the loan was received, and interest was used as a separate qualifier to explain the extra amount received relative to the principal. However, eventually, so many people began to accept these claims of *interest* as legitimate that hardly any loans for profit were considered usury anymore, and therefore the term interest just stuck, and usurious loans were only those that were considered "excessive". Now the fact that the word usury has shifted in meaning over time hardly seems debated, and the origins of this shift do not seem to be in dispute either. Where I would like to drill in though is how we seem to default to believing that the acceptance of "interest" in the form of compensatory payments for loans was and remains the appropriate thing to do. I believe if we pause to think through these different claims more rigorously, we will find that most of them that were used and those that continue to be used when pressed for debate, are quite weak.

One of the first exceptions was *damnum emergens*, meaning "damage accruing."[96] *Dammun emergens* would be claimed if there was some damage directly resulting from a lender making an otherwise gratuitous (free of charge) loan. For example, imagine that lender A loans borrower B $10,000 and expects to be repaid at

---

95 Mooney, *Usury: Destroyer of Nations*, 3.
96 Patrick Cleary, *The Church and Usury: An Essay on Some Historical and Theological Aspects of Money-Lending* (Dublin: M. H. Gill and Son, 1914), 92.

the end of the year. When borrower B could not pay back the loan, lender A unexpectedly came under hard times and had to take out a $1,000 loan at usury of 10% such that he paid $100 in interest. In this situation, lender A could claim damages of $100 due to borrower B not paying back on time and therefore use the *damnum emergens* title as justification for compensation of $100.

While I am not keen on many of the extrinsic titles that were claimed, *Damnum emergens* to me seems plausible that it could be claimed, especially if it relates to the fault or negligence of the borrower (e.g., late return of money). If you consider this title in its own right, namely that one party should have to compensate an aggrieved party for damages accrued as a result of the other party's actions, then this claim would not typically be debated. If I cause damages to my neighbor, then I should have to pay for those damages. While this extrinsic title has merit if used in good faith, the circumstances leading to a legitimate application of this title were rare historically and would be almost nonexistent today. It was not likely at any time in history that a loan would be made in good faith, not expecting to receive compensation for that loan, and that damage would accrue to the lender because of the borrower. Typically, those with the money to loan to others do not need it themselves. Hence, circumstances where the lack of repayment would lead to damages being accrued by the lender above and beyond the simple lack of repayment of the amount of money that was loaned were quite rare. If we considered this title in our modern context, I would consider it equally rare that someone would lend with the true intention of not profiting from a loan but would still end up accruing damages in some form due to the borrower's late payment or other acts.

One of the next exceptions commonly claimed was *lucrum cessans*, or "ceasing gain." *Lucrum cessans* is what we commonly think of as opportunity cost today or potential foregone profit from a missed opportunity. Of all the extrinsic titles claimed historically and that come up today in different discussions on usury, the widespread acceptance of this one puzzles me more than most. When claiming *lucrum cessans* on a $100 loan at 10% usury, what one is saying is $100 + $10 = $110, whereas the $100 is equivalent to the amount loaned, and the $10 is payment for what could have been done with the money had it not been loaned. Now, there's an initially obvious question of how you would know what you could have made with the money in other circumstances, but we can leave that presumption aside as that's not my main problem with this title.

Instead, I would like to reminisce about a time when I met a man named Joseph Edgar Foreman. It was our senior year at the University of Alabama, near the peak of my paganism, and we were preparing for our fraternity's biggest party. On a beautiful Friday afternoon in early Spring, I strolled across the parking lot near our house where the band playing that night had parked, and I reached out my hand to a rather unassuming, well-spoken man who introduced himself as Joseph. We exchanged pleasantries and confirmed the start time and anything else the band needed for the performance that night, and then we parted ways until the show.

When I saw Joseph later that night, it was like I was meeting an entirely different person. He had already fully transformed into the character of Afroman and was hardly recognizable from earlier in the day. Afroman put on quite the show, and he was certainly a crowd favorite, with everyone especially eager to hear his hit song "Because I Got High." In the song, the narrator melodically bemoans all the activities he could have done until he got high, of course. Most of the activities that the narrator failed to complete due to his getting high were quite laudable, such as cleaning his room or advancing in his profession. After reciting his failure to complete each activity, the narrator voices his half-hearted regret with airy and catchy "la de da's" to lead into the next activity that he fails to complete…because he got high, of course. Now, for all the things that could be said about the narrator in this song and his lack of motivation and inability to say no to his passions, he has at least one thing going for him - he has common sense. While the narrator may sing "I was gonna clean my room, until I got high,"[97] and lament the fact that "my room is still messed up, and I know why,"[98] at least he's not absurd enough to sing "I was gonna clean my room, until I got high…but cuz I could have, and chose not to, I know what I'll cry… with *lucrum cessans*, I, don't even try…and still get what's mine, still get what's mine, still get what's mine. La dee da da da".

Perhaps you may find my comparison strange, but I hope you will find the idea of the *lucrum cessans* title even stranger upon considering it more seriously. With the claim of *lucrum cessans*, or opportunity cost, as a justification for lending at interest, what we are saying is that $100 +$10 = $110. In this situation, the $100 is a

---

[97] "Because I Got High," Afroman, *Because I Got High*, T-Bones Records, 2000.
[98] "Because I Got High," Afroman.

return for an amount loaned, and the $10 is compensation due for what the lender could have done with the money but chose not to. Once you remove the $100 from the equation, you have $10 = what someone could have done with the money but otherwise chose not to. When is there ever another situation in our lives in which we would encourage someone to demand that they be compensated for something that they could have done but chose not to do? It would be absurd for the narrator in the song to have chosen to get high while also demanding a claim to a clean room on account of *lucrum cessans*. While it can be a fun thought exercise to debate how good Lebron James *could* have been if he was an NFL tight end or how great Tyreek Hill would have been as a soccer player, it would be absurd if Lebron James claimed *lucrum cessans* and demanded the Green Bay Packers pay him the salary he could have expected had he taken his talents to The Frozen Tundra instead of South Beach. And yet, this is the same thing as what we claim when we say that *lucrum cessans* is a justification for lending at usury. We are saying *lucrum cessans* is a valid claim, extrinsic to the agreement of the loan itself, such that on its own merits, one should be warranted compensation for something they could have done but chose not to do, under no compulsion whatsoever, but rather simply because they chose to do something different. This simply makes no sense, and hardly anyone would reason like this in any other aspect of their life, and yet, for whatever reason, when it comes to matters of money, we seem to shut off our critical thinking abilities such that we can almost universally and unreflectively consider that opportunity cost, or *lucrum cessans*, should be considered as a valid reason to lend money at interest.

Another common reason for charging interest on a loan today is that you are being justly compensated for the risk you are taking that you may not be repaid. This coincides with the extrinsic title of *periculum sortis*[99] that was debated at different times throughout the Middle Ages. Like the idea of *lucrum cessans*, the idea of being

---

[99] Much like with the word usury itself, there is significant development over the meaning of the phrase *periculum sortis*, throughout the history of the usury debate. Noonan describes this in the Scholastic Analysis of Usury on page 281: "*periculum sortis* customarily referred in medieval times only to the risk of capital borne by the borrower or by the lender acting as insurer, it now became the term to describe periculum mutui, the lender's risk in letting out his capital." So the risk that we intuitively think of with lending today, the risk that one may not receive their money back from the borrower, is what was originally meant by the phrase, *periculum mutui*, but eventually came to be referred to as *periculum sortis*. For the sake of simplicity, I will use the phrase *periculum sortis* to refer to the risk that the principal of the loan was not repaid.

compensated for the risk of non-payment often seems justified, but if you pause to think about it, the claims to this title fall just as short.

First off, as it relates to risk, you are typically not compensated for risk per se, but rather risk is something that you face in activities that may, but are not guaranteed, to result in a profit. If I start a farming venture, there is a chance the corn I plant will yield a substantial increase, and I can profit from this increase, but there is also a risk that my corn will not grow. The increase in the corn is the grounds for the profit, not the risk I took that the corn may not grow. If I pour gasoline on my crops and shoot fireworks towards them, there is a great risk that the crops will be damaged. Still, it is not as if the risk in and of itself is something worthy of compensation. You should rather consider the activity in and of itself and see if it is worth compensation. In this instance, it would be rather obvious that the activity of pouring gasoline on crops and shooting fireworks would not yield an increase or be worthy of profit. As it relates to lending money, assuming I lend $100, then the activity of that loan is worth exactly $100. The risk that I may not receive back $100, if taken on its own merit, is not worth anything, as risk alone is not worth compensation.

However, even if one does not buy the argument above, I think there's an easier way to prove that most money lending today would not warrant a claim to being compensated for risk. Most people today, whether banks or individual investors, lend because they want to receive more money than they lend out, plain and simple. This is a rather obvious statement few would dispute, yet one cannot truly claim they are only seeking compensation for the risk of non-payment of loans while also seeking profit from loans. If they only wanted to be compensated at an equivalent amount for the risk they were taking with their loans, then they would seek to break even, with the bad loans balancing out the good loans. Still, lending would not be a for-profit business endeavor, as by definition, in this type of business, you want to receive interest greater than what you lose due to nonpayment. In a small sample size, it may be difficult to gauge the impact of the risk of nonpayment such that you could truly be seeking compensation only for the risk of nonpayment and *accidentally* make a profit. However, a professional money lender or an institutional investor could easily balance their lending and interest rates such that they only received back in interest the *equivalent* of what they lost due to nonpayment, not more than they would lose due to nonpayment.

And finally, even if the above are not compelling as it relates to risk, please do not deceive yourself into thinking that the primary money lenders of today in the banking system are taking risks. Most banks in our current system are not taking any risks when they make a loan - they are creating money through the act of the loan, so it is not as if they are risking money they had, they are "risking" money they created through the process of the loan.

The next justification for discussion is the common claim that lending at interest may be sinful for *consumption* loans, but this must be fine for *productive* or business loans. There are several reasons that I believe this exception falls short, but before diving into these reasons, historical context could help in understanding this exception. The 15th and 16th centuries mark a notable period where the views of the sinfulness of usury were whittled down in two prominent locations: Germany and Italy. We will dive into the Italian developments in more detail shortly, but for the time being, I would like to discuss the notable developments in Germany in the 16th century relating to the *contractus trinus, or* triple contract. The triple contract was a series of contracts that claimed to enable individuals to lend at a moderate interest rate without running afoul of the sin or scandal of usury, and these arrangements became quite popular in Germany at this time.[100]

Here are how these arrangements worked. Suppose you have businessman B and lender L. Businessman B and lender L enter into three different agreements. With Agreement 1 - B & L enter a *societas* agreement, essentially the same as a business partnership, where risk and reward are shared in some capacities in the partnership. In this agreement, L has capital to provide, and B has labor to provide, so L gives B $1000, and B agrees to do work leveraging this capital investment, and they agree to split the rewards. Assuming they make an expected $300 profit, L would receive $1150 ($150 or 15% profit) and B would receive $150. If the venture lost money and only made $800, L would receive $800, a loss of $200 or 20%.

With agreement 2, B & L enter into an insurance agreement. In this agreement, L (the one providing the capital to the partnership) seeks to have his principal insured against the risk of loss by B. So, L pays a fee to B to have L's $1000 principal insured. Instead of

---

[100] Hoffman, *Usury in Christendom*, 171.

paying the fee directly, the fee is paid as a cap on the profit L would receive from the partnership. For example, if the partnership made $300 profit, instead of L receiving $1150 ($150 profit + original investment), L would only receive $120 profit at 12%, and B would receive $180 profit. If the venture lost money, though, and only $800 remained from the principal investment, then L would receive the $1000 principal back, and B would have a $200 loss.

With agreement 3 - B & L enter another insurance agreement where an uncertain future gain is sold for a lesser certain gain. Before agreement 3, L is providing $1000 capital and can receive at most $120 (or 12%) profit, but he will receive at least his $1000 back, and B has no cap on the profit he can receive, but he must at least return $1000 to L. With agreement 3, L sells a portion of his uncertain future gain (12% return) to B for a lesser certain gain, such that L now caps his profit at 5% on the partnership, but he is also guaranteed a 5% return on the partnership no matter the results. B must now return $1050 to L (5% greater than the amount invested) no matter the venture's results.

The astute reader may think this agreement looks like lender L just loaned to businessman B at a rate of 5% interest, and I would say the reader who thinks this is correct. The aggregate result of these combined agreements is the same as a 5% loan at interest, which seems like usury. To borrow from the Southerner's translation of Occam's razor - if it looks like a duck, quacks like a duck, and smells like a duck…it's probably a duck. But why would anyone go through all the trouble to have this convoluted triple agreement set up? Why would Lender L not just lend to Borrower B at 5% interest? At this time in history, the idea of usury was still quite scandalous, so these contracts were put in place so that the appearance of usury could be shrouded. Individuals could essentially provide loans at interest while their consciences and reputations could remain untroubled.

In modern times the sentiments around usury have changed such that the theatrics around these complex agreements are not necessary for those seeking to lend at interest while keeping their reputations intact; however, the main impetus behind the triple contract then and common arguments for interest today in this regard have remained unchanged. Many of the arguments in favor of the triple contract were essentially economic.[101] These loans were just so good for the economy! How could something that feels so right possibly be wrong? And today you have similar arguments. Some may think that "consumption loans," or those not used to pursue a business endeavor, could be considered harmful and usurious, but how could someone fault a lender for providing capital to a business to spur growth? The bankers are just business partners, right? In these instances, doesn't everyone win? The borrower can turn the debt into an even greater profit while providing a valuable service to the community, and the lender can receive a reasonable return on her investment.

Regarding the evidence from scripture, you certainly do not find anything supporting such a distinction. As already discussed, scripture consistently condemns usury in general, with a specific emphasis on not exacting usury from the poor, and provides only one qualification when exacting usury would be licit from an enemy in the promised land Israel was set to conquer. Out of all the scripture on usury, you would have to squint hard to try and see anything germane to the distinction between business loans vs consumption loans. However, distinguishing between these two categories of loans was not an idea the different writers of scripture had in mind at the time of writing, so I do not think it would be fair to dismiss this idea outright simply because scripture does not directly address it.

There are several other challenges with trying to use this exception as justification, though. The first is the arbitrary distinction between "consumption loans" and "productive loans." Suppose one man takes out a loan to buy a car for personal use, and another takes out a loan to buy a car to be an Uber driver. Is there such a difference between these two types of loans in any meaningful way such that one is morally condemned, and the other is morally licit? Both are being used to purchase the same thing. I suspect one might say that in the situation of the Uber driver, or in any other scenario where the loan is of a reasonable amount to support a business, it's a "win-win" situation, and since no harm is done and all benefit, then, therefore, this is not wrong. But that's not really what happens in these situations. First off, in the scenario of a business loan, the borrower benefits from the *loan*, not the *usury*. That may seem rather obvious, but it's an important distinction. The

---

[101] Noonan. *Scholastic Analysis of Usury*, 210.

loan itself is a good thing, and it is not surprising that good can and often does result from someone with more than they need lending to someone with less than they need. However, the loan conditions that require the borrower to pay back more than they borrowed are certainly not good for the borrower. And even in a scenario when the borrower makes a profit great enough to pay back the lender the principal and the usury, the damage of the usury still occurs, it is just diffused through society in the form of higher prices the borrower must charge for their business endeavor to generate enough profit for themselves and to cover the usury they owe the lender. Someone may then try to counter that the incentive of interest is necessary; otherwise, no one may be willing to lend to the borrower. But this type of argument fails with Christians in almost every other scenario. Aquinas puts this succinctly and directly in teaching that the ends do not justify the means,[102] and most Christians intuitively understand that you ought not to do bad things even if they are seeking a good outcome. If one is to argue otherwise, one should know that one is on the side of Machiavelli, who unashamedly teaches that the ends justify the means,[103] not with Christ. In summary, I believe the claim should be rejected that business loans are distinct from productive loans as it relates to the morality of lending at interest. These should be treated the same in this regard - either sinful or licit, as there are no compelling reasons to treat them distinctly.

Part 5: The Catholic Church's Stance on Usury

As we have discussed the rise of the triple contracts in Germany, now is a good time to turn our attention to another consequential historical trend that contributed to the current state of usury, with the *mons pietatis* rising throughout Italy in the 15th century. The *mons pietatis* were lending institutions stated to provide loans at low rates of interest to the poor, which, if taken at face value, sounds potentially laudable. However, the circumstances surrounding their rise and the theological responses to the controversy surrounding these institutions certainly offer reason to be skeptical of their stated good intentions. The most compelling arguments in favor of these

---

[102] *The Catechism of the Catholic Church,* 1759, http://www.scborromeo.org/ccc/para/1759.htm
[103] Nicolo Machiavelli, *The Prince,* Chapter XV, https://www.gutenberg.org/files/1232/1232-h/1232-h.htm

institutions appealed to the title of *damnum emergens*, stating that the interest charged by the institutions only covered the expenses necessary to run them.[104] If this is indeed how these were run, and they were not a subterfuge to gather a profit through loans in the name of charity, then it would be hard to argue against this position. Using the simplistic way we have been looking at these situations to understand these extrinsic titles, if a loan of $10 requires repayment of $11, whereas $11 equals the $10 principal, plus $1 for expenses incurred by the venture, then if you subtract the $10 from both sides of the equation, then you have the $1 compensation by itself representing the expenses incurred. To charge someone for expenses or damages that one incurred is a reasonable thing and typically not argued against in other scenarios. I would suggest it would warrant repayment if these were truly expenses incurred. Whether or not that was the case with these *Montes Pietatis*, I believe, is a tough question to answer.

Unsurprisingly, the historical references on these institutions seem to slant according to the view of the writer presenting the information, with those who have an unfavorable view of usury highlighting the case against these institutions operating as generously as stated. In contrast, those who believe the evolution of the views on the morality of usury as a positive thing will highlight the charitable aspects of these institutions. It would take a historical scholar much greater than myself to sort through the truth on the workings of these institutions, but whether these institutions acted maliciously is not the primary reason I bring them up. Rather, I find the responses to these institutions interesting as they raise important theological questions relating to the Christian tradition's teaching on usury. As mentioned earlier in this book, all Christian tradition stood clearly and firmly against usury for at least the first 1,300 years after Christ. While the definition of usury was often implicitly assumed, where it was defined, it was consistently defined as expecting to receive any amount greater than what was lent. However, with Pope Leo X, otherwise known as Giovanni di Lorenzo de' Medici of the Medici banking dynasty, you have one of the first papal writings that suggest nuance to the views on usury relative to the historical position. In the Fifth Lateran Council of 1515, which was led by Pope Leo X, the council ultimately affirms the *Mons Pietatis* as the council records the following: "Since, therefore, this whole question appears to concern the peace and tranquility of the whole christian state, we declare and define, with

---

[104] Cleary, *The Church and Usury*, 111.

the approval of the sacred council, that the above-mentioned credit organizations, established by states and hitherto approved and confirmed by the authority of the apostolic see, do not introduce any kind of evil or provide any incentive to sin if they receive, in addition to the capital, a moderate sum for their expenses and by way of compensation, provided it is intended exclusively to defray the expenses of those employed and of other things pertaining (as mentioned) to the upkeep of the organizations, and provided that no profit is made therefrom. They ought not, indeed, to be condemned in any way."[105] So, in this particular statement, the Pope is only approving a narrow exception where more money could be received than the amount loaned without it being considered usury, provided that the additional amount received above and beyond the loan amount is used to cover expenses and no profit is obtained. While this is a rather narrow exception, it still represents a shift in the general sentiments around usury in Christian teachings compared with just a few centuries prior.

However, earlier in the writing from this same council, Pope Leo X makes a statement that I believe to be more consequential and debatably veering from the historical position on usury when he says, "For, that is the real meaning of usury: when, from its use, a thing which produces nothing is applied to the acquiring of gain and profit without any work, any expense or any risk."[106] Most non-Catholics would probably care little about this statement. Since I am not a Catholic myself, I hope to only gingerly dip my toes into what I know could drop to deep water rather quickly. Still, since we have gone this far with the research on this topic, and one of my secondary arguments for why I believe usury should still be considered a sin relates to the teaching from Christian tradition, I see no way to avoid trying to make sense of how we got from there in the tradition to here in modernity.

As I understand the Catholic view, and coming from the catechism itself, the magisterium of the church informs how the Pope and the collection of bishops supporting the Pope have been entrusted by Jesus Christ as the ultimate authority to interpret Christian doctrine. "The task of giving an authentic interpretation of the Word of God, whether in its written form or in the form of Tradition, has been

---

[105] *Papal Encyclicals Online,* "Fifth Lateran Council 1512-17 A. D.'"
https://www.papalencyclicals.net/councils/ecum18.htm
[106] *Papal Encyclicals Online,* "Fifth Lateran Council 1512-17 A. D.'"
https://www.papalencyclicals.net/councils/ecum18.htm

entrusted to the living teaching office of the Church alone. Its authority in this matter is exercised in the name of Jesus Christ." This means that the task of interpretation has been entrusted to the bishops in communion with the successor of Peter, the Bishop of Rome."[107]

The debates and true meaning of this idea become exceedingly difficult to follow, especially regarding whether the Church is allowed to change her teaching on key topics. My understanding of the reason this view holds such importance is that if the Church claims to be the ultimate interpreter of complex doctrinal debates, and decides one way on a doctrinal issue and then later changes its position on that same doctrinal issue, then one could say the Church contradicted herself, and therefore proves that she is not the ultimate interpreter of doctrinal issues, since one of her interpretations must have been wrong. However, what exactly constitutes dogma or established doctrine within the Catholic Church, who within the Catholic Church holds preeminence in establishing these views, and what constitutes a *development* of dogma (i.e., a greater understanding of truth revealed through the generations) as opposed to a *changing* of dogma (i.e., teaching something different than what was previously taught) continues to be debated by those much more qualified than me to weigh in on the matter. While I have immense respect for the Catholic Church and have seen too much evidence of God working through the lives of those within the Catholic Church today and throughout the recorded history of the saints of the Church to dismiss these ideas hastily, I am not Catholic. Therefore, I do not believe these tenets of the Catholic faith that are unique to this denomination. Therefore I view the Roman Catholic Church as one branch of many, as opposed to a branch set apart with unique access to the fullest extent of God's grace through the sacraments, and while I believe that those under the care of the Roman Catholic Church will bear much fruit, provided they abide in the True Vine, I do not doubt that those who are members of other congregations will bear much fruit, provided they abide in the True Vine as well.

Some acknowledgment of this context seemed necessary before continuing on with the discussion from tradition, as an obvious question arises when it appears that Christian tradition used to think

---

[107] *The Catechism of the Catholic Church,* 85, https://www.catholiccrossreference.online/catechism/#!/search/85-87

usury was a sin and now no longer considers this a sin. Most will be wondering, "What happened"? When humans try to make sense of complex historical events to understand how we arrive at a current situation, we are undoubtedly prone to fill in as much of the narrative we believe from our presuppositions as we are with carefully curated evidence. I must remain on guard to this fallible heuristic as much as the next guy. As mentioned towards the beginning of the chapter, you have a wealth of evidence from the first 1,300 years of the Christian tradition where several councils and notable fathers of the faith spoke against usury, where usury meant asking for more than was lent. The definition of usury was often implied, but in every instance where the definition was detailed, the explanation was that usury meant asking for more than was lent, typically in loans of money, but not fully limited to this arrangement. St. Ambrose defines usury as extorting *more than one has given.* You have St. Augustine defining usury as if *thou hast given the loan of thy money to one from whom thou dost expect to receive something more than thou hast given. St. Thomas Aquinas defines* usury as "to take payment for the use of money lent, which payment is known as usury", to name a few.[108] While I know absence of evidence does not prove evidence of absence, I could not find counter examples of reputable Christian voices who spoke against this view of usury during this time, and the point that Christian tradition spoke against usury for centuries, and viewed usury as expecting more than was lent rarely seems to be debated.

Around the 14th through 18th centuries though, you find a renewed interest in the usury debate, with most of the debates surrounding the different exceptions discussed above. This situation seems similar in many ways to theological and ethical debates common to our time, such as those around same-sex relationships, where ideas that for much of Christian history were unchallenged and perhaps seemed straightforward, suddenly came under much more scrutiny, especially as the moral norms of the world changed around the Church. With usury, for at least several centuries after Aquinas and the heyday of the scholastic period, you would not find theologians to challenge the meaning of usury; however, you would find many challenges suggesting that the different extrinsic titles such as *damnun emergens, lucrum cessans, or periculum sortis,* should be accepted as exceptions to loan arrangements and therefore should not be considered usury. As stated above, I think nearly all these

---

[108] *New Advent,* Aquinas, Summa Theologia, Question 78, Article 1, https://www.newadvent.org/summa/3078.htm

extrinsic titles should be rejected, except perhaps *damnun emergens*, which, if taken in the proper spirit, should apply rather infrequently to loan arrangements and not materially impact the usury debate. However, with Pope Leo X, you do find this statement that certainly seems to suggest a changing definition of usury, when he speaks of the "real meaning" of usury, "when, from its use, a thing which produces nothing is applied to the acquiring of gain and profit without any work, any expense or any risk."[109] What precisely Leo X means by "without any work, any expense, or any risk," I am sure could, and probably has been, debated ad nauseam, but this certainly seems to present rather strong footing for one wanting to skirt the condemnation of usury, as one could easily take rather general views of the meaning of these phrases and consider many loan arrangements to require some risk, especially assuming you meant risk to mean the chance not to receive back what one lent.[110]

So if we take this back to the whole Catholic Church teaching question, what's not in dispute is that you have a Pope from the family of one of the most prominent banking dynasties in all of Europe at the time, the Medici Family, who interprets a narrow issue around lending at usury in favor of specific *Mons Pietatis* lending institutions and makes statements about lending in general that broadens the loans where one could licitly demand more in payment than was loaned. What would be disputed is whether this statement represents a *change* in teaching, which I think would be considered a big "no-no" for the church, or whether this represents a

---

[109] *Papal Encyclicals Online,* "Fifth Lateran Council 1512-17 A. D.,"
https://www.papalencyclicals.net/councils/ecum18.htm
[110] Noonan, to his credit, addresses this consideration in *The Scholastic Analysis of Usury* head-on. Per Noonan, although Catholic writers subsequent to Pope Leo X interpreted this statement on risk to refer to the risk that principal would not have been repaid, Noonan considers that anachronistic as that interpretation of the title to risk was not something considered by theologians at this time. Noonan writes in page 283: "Clearly, what it means by "periculum" is "periculum sortis" in the medieval sense, the risk assumed by an investor in a partnership; for this is the only kind of risk that would normally have been understood as a possible excuse by any theologian of the period, and we cannot suppose that the bull meant to use the word in a different sense from the common theological one." What precisely one thinks Pope Leo X meant by the word risk (and whether it even matters what he meant by this word) will probably be informed as much by one's presuppositions on other theological matters such as the Magisterium of the Church as anything else. In Noonan's explanation on the matter, he even outright states the presupposition that "we cannot suppose that the bull meant to use the word in a different sense from the common theological one". But why not? If one believes the teaching authority of Christ was truly given to the Catholic Church, then perhaps we must agree with Noonan, but if one does not believe that in the same sense that Roman Catholics do, then it seems entirely plausible that a Medici Pope could have said something different about usury compared to many of his theological peers of the time.

development in dogma around usury without any change in the teaching. Again, I am not Catholic, so I do not have a dogma in this fight, and if my convictions relating to usury are correct, none of us should look to usury for evidence of denominational superiority as almost all of us have caved on this matter. Protestants have our weekly Bible studies and repeated exhortations to stay entrenched in the Scriptures, and while many of us really do these things, we somehow repeatedly gloss over this uncomfortable, but quite obvious truth, staring us right in the face over and over again in the Scriptures. And while Catholics have this beautiful commitment to Church tradition, they seem to conveniently gloss over centuries of consistent condemnations of usury.

For what it's worth to anyone who may be pressed to reconcile these ideas around usury with an understanding of the Catholic Church's historical teaching compared to the current state of the Church's teaching, there seem to be several different paths one could take. One of course would be to reject the idea that dogma does not change. This is the path Michael Hoffman takes in his book on usury, where he writes, "While it is often said that the dogma of the Roman Catholic Church is unchanging, truth to tell, the Renaissance Church did overthrow the dogma on usury. This is disputed by many eminent Catholics; sad to say, they are in error. From the earliest period, the whole weight of the Church was brought to bear against *all* gain made from lending - not just on "unjust" interest."[111] One could also double down on the fact that the Church never changes her teaching and treat the statements from Pope Leo X as a development of dogma. This is the path that Noonan seems to take in his book on usury, "Moreover, as far as dogma in the technical Catholic sense is concerned, there is only one dogma at stake. Dogma is not to be loosely used as synonymous with every papal rule or theological verdict. Dogma is a defined, revealed doctrine taught by the Church at all times and places. Nothing here meets the test of dogma except this assertion, that usury, the act of taking profit on a loan without a just title, is sinful. Even this dogma is not specifically, formally defined by any pope or council. It is, however, taught by the tradition of the Church, as witnessed by papal bulls and briefs, conciliar acts, and theological opinion. This dogmatic teaching remains unchanged. What is a just title, what is technically to be treated as a loan, are matters of debate, positive law, and changing evaluation. The

---

[111] Hoffman, *Usury in Christendom*, 62.

development on these points is great. But the pure and narrow dogma is the same today as in 1200"[112] If one takes the development of dogma approach, I think there is rather wide latitude in how one could view modern lending practices at interest. I am unaware of the title of *lucrum cessans* explicitly being deemed licit or illicit in papal writings, and if one accepted many of the extrinsic titles such as *lucrum cessans* (essentially opportunity cost) and *periculum sortis* (compensation for risk), then you could salve your conscience by viewing much of lending at interest in the modern world as being justified on these grounds. If one rejected these titles, then I could see how one could still hold to the idea that the Catholic Church does not change her teaching by thinking that most lending today would *not* be justified on the grounds of extrinsic titles and therefore we have just mostly ignored the truth that lending at interest is a sin. As mentioned in the footnote above, there are also good reasons put forth by Noonan to imagine a different interpretation of the claims about "without risk" made by Pope Leo X such that this does not apply to the nearly universal and intrinsic risk of a loan not being repaid, but rather relates to another narrower interpretation of risk dealing with partnership arrangements.

Catholic teachings subsequent to Pope Leo X such as *Vix Pervenit* by Pope Benedict XIV in 1745, do seem to reconfirm the historical definition of usury as meaning when someone demands more from a loan than was given, which does further complicate the question around whether the church changed her teaching. In the first paragraph of *Vix Pervenit*, the last papal writing to thoroughly and directly address usury, the definition of usury seems to be different from that of Pope Leo X, but reconfirmed as the same as the consensus of Christian history for almost its entire existence as Benedict XIV writes, "The nature of the sin called usury has its proper place and origin in a loan contract. This financial contract between consenting parties demands, by its very nature, that one return to another only as much as he has received. The sin rests on the fact that sometimes the creditor desires more than he has given. Therefore he contends some gain is owed him beyond that which he loaned, but any gain which exceeds the amount he gave is illicit and usurious."[113]

The rest of *Vix Pervenit* offers several direct refutations of common

---

[112] Noonan, Scholastic Analysis of Usury, 399-400.
[113] *Papal Encyclicals Online*, "Vix Pervenit: On Usury and Other Dishonest Profits," https://www.papalencyclicals.net/ben14/b14vixpe.htm

exceptions that were and sometimes still are claimed but still leaves many questions about the Catholic view of certain extrinsic titles up in the air. The second point of the third paragraph states that one "cannot condone the sin of usury by arguing that the gain is not great or excessive,"[114] "by arguing that the borrower is rich," "nor even by arguing that the money borrowed is not left idle, but is spent usefully."[115] The third point of this same paragraph however is followed up with "By these remarks, however, We do not deny that at times together with the loan contract certain other titles-which are not at all intrinsic to the contract-may run parallel with it. From these other titles, entirely just and legitimate reasons arise to demand something over and above the amount due on the contract."[116] And in the sixth paragraph, Benedict expands this idea when he says, "Concerning the specific contract which caused these new controversies, We decide nothing for the present; We also shall not decide now about the other contracts in which the theologians and canonists lack agreement."[117]

While there are still some writings for or against usury after *Vix Pervenit*, the whole fight seemed to trickle down to a whimper up to our modern day. While the usury apologists never presented some earth-shattering answer that made sense of how such a change in the view of usury against the Scriptures and the tradition of the Christian church could be reconciled, or at least not one that I could ever find that made sense to me, the general practice and acceptance from the public of lending at interest continued such that it never seemed to matter. Our itching ears usually do not seek truth; rather, we just want someone to tell us what we want to hear. All it took was a few voices to proclaim certain extrinsic titles as justifying lending at interest for us to turn off our critical thinking as to whether these titles should be considered valid while ignoring the rest of the vast evidence against usury. Distraction has always proved to be a better weapon for the devil than engaging the intellect.

---

[114] *Papal Encyclicals Online*, "Vix Pervenit: On Usury and Other Dishonest Profits," https://www.papalencyclicals.net/ben14/b14vixpe.htm
[115] *Papal Encyclicals Online*, "Vix Pervenit: On Usury and Other Dishonest Profits," https://www.papalencyclicals.net/ben14/b14vixpe.htm
[116] *Papal Encyclicals Online*, "Vix Pervenit: On Usury and Other Dishonest Profits," https://www.papalencyclicals.net/ben14/b14vixpe.htm
[117] *Papal Encyclicals Online*, "Vix Pervenit: On Usury and Other Dishonest Profits," https://www.papalencyclicals.net/ben14/b14vixpe.htm

Part 6: Remaining Arguments from Modernity Against Usury

While the extrinsic titles mentioned thus far represent most of the key points from when this was still a thriving theological issue, there are still a few more examples that are common today left to address. The most common remaining argument left undiscussed relates to the time value of money, which states that money in the present should be valued greater than money to be received in the future. With the theory of the time value of money, the common argument is that taking interest on a loan is justified because this is just compensation for the difference in the present value of money compared to the future value of money. So, the argument goes, if I loan someone $100 and expect to receive $110 a year from now, the $10 difference should be justified as it represents the difference between the future value of the money and its present amount. However, when you dig into this theory further, it still does not present a compelling case to justify usury.

Baked into the time value of money theory are assumptions on why present money should be worth more than future money. When considering why present money could be worth more than future money, there are only 4 options. Option 1 - present money of an amount is worth more than future money of that same amount because present money could be grown through profitable investment in a business of some sort, option 2 - present money of an amount is worth more than future money of that same amount because present money could be grown by making loans at interest, option 3 - present money of an amount is worth more than future money of that same amount because of a subjective preference to have something now as opposed to later, and option 4 - present money of an amount is worth more than future money of the same amount because inflation will have decreased the purchasing power of money in the future relative to the present. If we take these options in turn, only one warrants serious consideration for justifying usury.

With option 1, you have the same argument for *lucrum cessans*, or opportunity cost, under the banner of time value of money, which I have already discussed and dismissed as a valid extrinsic title earlier. Option 2's higher present value presupposes lending at interest, which is the question at hand, so this option for the time value of money cannot justify usury. With option 3, a subjective preference cannot override an objective reality related to matters of justice. The philosophical claims against usury are that it is an injustice because when one exacts usury, you are charging both for something and its use in situations where you cannot do both, and this presents an unjust inequality in the agreement. As stated in Aquinas's summary on this matter, "wherefore in such like things the use of the thing must not be reckoned apart from the thing itself, and whoever is granted the use of the thing, is granted the thing itself and for this reason, to lend things of this kind is to transfer the ownership."[118] The nature of money is such that it is consumed upon its use, which would be its transfer in the loan agreement, so it is theoretically impossible to charge both for money and its use. The just charge for money itself is money - $100 equals $100 - and you cannot charge for using money in a loan agreement in addition to money itself because you are then charging for something that is not yours. When you loan money, you consume it, and the person who receives the loan then owns that money - the agreement is just to receive an amount back equivalent to what you lent out, not to receive the exact same money itself. A subjective preference cannot outweigh an objective reality in morals within the Christian worldview. Further to point against the idea of a subjective preference towards money in the present over money in the future justifying usury, if someone in the position to make a loan truly had such a greater subjective preference over money in the present compared to money in the future, then why would he make the loan? If someone wants the money in the present so badly, then just don't make a loan - no one is being compelled to make these loans.

While options 1, 2, and 3 can be dismissed rather quickly relating to whether the time value of money can justify usury, I find it hard to reject an argument relating to inflation completely. With inflation, which is rather widely understood and discussed in detail earlier, you have a decrease in the purchasing power of money due to an increase in the money supply. In situations of inflation, your money today is objectively worth more than your money will be worth in the future. In periods of inflation, one hundred dollars today will buy more bananas than one hundred dollars a year from now. Therefore, if someone loans $100 today and that $100 could buy 100 bananas, and that person expects to receive only an equivalent of the same value of money back in the future, this could be a higher amount of money as each dollar in the future may be worth

---

[118] *New Advent*, Aquinas, *Summa Theologia*, Second Part of the Second Part, Question 78, Article 1, https://www.newadvent.org/summa/3078.htm

less than each dollar was at the time of the loan. It may take $110 to buy 100 bananas by the time the loan is repaid, and therefore, a good argument could be made that in these situations, a just equivalence is maintained in the transaction.

Before anyone rushes off to celebrate, thinking that we have found an appropriate and ubiquitous exception so we can go back to ignoring usury like we have been for the last few centuries, a few caveats are in order. First, please do not consider that inflation concerns justify the source of most loans today, which come from the banking system. Remember, when banks loan money, they create money through the loan process; they are not loaning money they already have. They are creating inflation; they are not the victims of inflation. Additionally, for those individuals or institutions who are loaning existing money they have and not creating money as a part of their loan agreement, whether it be through bonds or some other type of loan arrangement, if they are loaning money and expect only to be compensated to cover the cost of inflation, then they still ought to have an intention behind the loan to truly not profit from the arrangement, but only to break even when considering inflation. I will not know how many who engage in these loans only seek repayment as an equivalent to inflation. However, I suspect it to be low as the default moral position of the day is to unashamedly seek as much growth as possible with your money through investment, with lending at interest being considered a reputable way to invest one's money. While I would consider accounting for inflation to be an appropriate justification for lending at interest for some loans that do not create money as part of the loan and are not seeking a profit beyond the amount of inflation, the applicability of these situations should be narrowly and cautiously applied.

The last argument that I find justifying interest today usually comes from Catholics trying to reconcile claims that the Church changed her teaching on usury relative to her historical position by stating something to the effect that doctrine or dogma never changed, but rather our understanding of the nature and function of money changed in modern times. To the credit of Catholics, they at least seem to be bothered enough by this question of usury to engage with it more frequently than Protestants, who typically just bulldoze through any questions on the matter with blissful indifference. Still, I find this argument that the function and nature of money has changed weak at best and frightening at worst. For those who make this argument, I have yet to find one who expounds on what exactly they think the essence or nature of money used to be and what exactly they think the essence or nature of money is now. Still, they usually gingerly reference things such as opportunity cost or the time value of money as concepts that we understand better now that justify lending at interest. As I have already discussed why I do not believe these justify usury, I will not elaborate on them further here. Still, I would like to provide thorough consideration to the argument that the nature of money changed, and perhaps even more so than is usually given by those who casually throw out phrases such as these without bothering to explain what they mean by them.

As I pondered the question, "What is the nature of money?" I found it surprisingly difficult to answer. In an earlier section of this book, we discussed money using Aristotle's four causes, the material cause (what something is made of), the efficient cause (what causes something to exist), and the final cause (the ultimate purpose of an object), however I did not include much to the discussion relating to money's formal cause (the essence of the thing itself), which is now the question at hand. I did not include much around the formal cause of money as it's not something we typically include in conversations around money, and I can hardly find any resource that ever speaks to the quiddity of money (what money actually *is*). Casual searches for the definition of money will usually just reference what money does (its final cause), such as serving as a medium of exchange or a store of value, and what money is made of (its material cause), such as gold or paper. Money's efficient cause, faith, will sometimes be discussed; however, I could not find a single definition that speaks about money itself. I am not sure who first said this to credit this quote properly, but I have seen it cleverly quipped that "money is what money does." Regarding this phenomenon, we still struggle to understand what money actually *is*. Therefore, we say that it is what it does.

Perhaps I have missed definitions that speak to the essence of money, but since I have struggled to find this information from other sources, I have included what I think the essence of money is for the sake of this argument. To me, the essence, or formal cause of money, or what uniquely makes money money, is that money is anything that is a quantitative representation of value independent of itself. For example, when economies gravitate towards a certain item that begins to be used as money, whether that be shells, cigarettes, gold, or cryptocurrency, the thing that becomes money does so when it quantifies value separately from the thing itself, and it remains money if it continues to do so. Suppose seashells happen to turn into money in an economy. In that case, they are no longer valued because of whatever intrinsic worth exists in seashells or for whatever function seashells can serve. Still, they are valued because they quantitatively represent the value of what the seashells could be traded for. The same goes for something like gold or silver. While I know gold and silver have some value as semiconductors or to be used to make silverware, when gold and silver turn into money, they are no longer valued primarily for the intrinsic uses of the metal, but rather, they are valued because they quantitatively represent the value of the other items they could be traded for. The same goes for cryptocurrency and whatever form of money you could think of.

Using this definition of the essence of money, a quantitative representation of value independent of itself, the essence of money has not changed in modern times, and I do not think it has ever changed. Today, our monetary system is a credit and debt-based system. Whatever little money I have in my bank account today is simply an aggregation of credits that have been partitioned into tiny slivers from their corresponding debts and traded amongst numerous parties in the economy before landing with me. The essence of this modern money is that my credit is a quantitative representation of the value of the goods and services that it could be traded for within our economy. It is not valued in and of itself. Take whatever money that has existed throughout the history of the world, whether that be gold, silver, cryptocurrency, or whatever has been used as money. The essence of the money will be the same - it is a quantitative representation of the goods and services it could be traded for within its economy; it is not valued in and of itself.

Therefore, I reject the argument that usury is no longer a sin because of the nature or essence of money changing, as the nature or essence of money has not changed. I find it quite frightening how quickly we are prone to believe this argument, as it seems to presuppose a shocking elevation of our idolatry of money from something we adore to something we deify. Signs point to things, but they are not the things themselves. If you are eagerly anticipating a vacation to the beach, but weary of your travels, and you decide to stop at the green sign that says "Beach - 100 miles", hoping that it will serve as a nice consolation to your intended destination, you will of course be sorely disappointed. Money is primarily a sign - it points to other things. Money in and of itself can do nothing - it cannot grow, it cannot nourish, and it certainly cannot save you - and yet despite these commonsensical limitations of money, it is common parlance to describe money as fertile today, which I suppose people say to mean that money *itself* can grow or bear fruit or bring life. This is just not what happens, and it is absurd to think it is. When a business is profitable, money does not grow. The money used to run the business is consumed to pay people who provide labor or buy materials transformed into products worth selling or machines that help make labor more effective. When the business grows and receives more money than when it started, they do this because someone else pays more money to receive the transformed materials or the benefits of the services the business offers compared to the combined costs of the materials and labor.

Nowhere in these interactions, though, is money fertile. Money is not like an acorn that achieves its perfection as a full-grown oak tree. In each interaction used to sustain and grow the business; money is consumed when it is used for labor or materials. When the first laborer is hired, the money does not grow into the laborer, and when the first materials are purchased, the money does not transform into the material. The money is traded for these things, and then whatever fertile growth appears within the business results from the labor and the materials, not the money itself.

And yet, while all of this should be so obvious if we pause to think about it, we have so deified money that we act as if the breath of life comes from it. We have mistaken the effect for the cause. Money is nothing but the creation of man, and if left in its proper place, it could perhaps be considered a fine and beneficial creation; however, when we look to money as our sustaining providence, we are in trouble. Money remains only because it is sustained by man's faith - we breathe life into money, but we have adored this thing for so long that we seem to believe that money sustains man. We certainly have not changed much from our ancestors in the time of Isaiah's writing.

"All who make idols are nothing, and the things they treasure are worthless. Those who would speak up for them are blind; they are ignorant, to their own shame. Who shapes a god and casts an idol, which can profit nothing? People who do that will be put to shame; such craftsmen are only human beings. Let them all come together and take their stand; they will be brought down to terror and shame. The blacksmith takes a tool and works with it in the coals; he shapes an idol with hammers, he forges it with the might of his arm. He gets hungry and loses his strength; he drinks no water and grows faint. The carpenter measures with a line and makes an outline with a marker; he roughs it out with chisels and marks it with compasses. He shapes it in human form, human form in all its glory, that it may dwell in a shrine. He cut down cedars, or perhaps took a cypress or oak. He let it grow among the trees of the forest, or planted a pine, and the rain made it grow. It is used as fuel for burning; some of it he takes and warms himself, he kindles a fire and bakes bread. But he also fashions a god and worships it; he makes an idol and bows down to it. Half of the wood he burns in the fire; over it he prepares his meal, he roasts his meat and eats his fill. He also warms himself and says, "Ah! I am warm; I see the fire." From the rest he makes a god, his idol; he bows down to it and worships. He prays to it and says, "Save me! You are my god!" They know nothing, they understand nothing; their eyes are plastered over so they cannot see, and their minds closed so they cannot understand" (Isaiah 44:9-18).

So it is with us. We grow weary with our tireless work, constantly shaping and maintaining our idol, and yet we foolishly look to the thing we are perpetually sustaining for rest and salvation.

Now, before wrapping this section up, I would like to discuss a few final miscellaneous questions and common misconceptions I hear and suspect the reader may also have. The first relates to whether it is a sin to borrow at interest. While it may perhaps be unwise to borrow from others at interest, in most situations, I do not believe it is a sin from the borrower's perspective if they take out a loan at interest, provided it is for a good reason. I take this position for several reasons.

For starters, scripture never condemns borrowing at interest; it simply condemns lending at interest. The closest you could find suggesting otherwise would be to quote Proverbs 22:7[119], stating: "The rich rules over the poor, and the borrower is the slave of the lender." I could envision an argument stating that entering into bondage such as this is making you a slave to something other than righteousness and, therefore, sinful. However, I think that is a stretch because the main thrust of this verse still seems to be

---

[119] *English Standard Version.*

primarily focused on the wrongs of the rich or lender in this situation, especially considering the subsequent two verses after this one "Whoever sows injustice will reap calamity, and the rod of his fury will fail. Whoever has a bountiful eye will be blessed, for he shares his bread with the poor." Proverbs 22:8-9[120]

Additionally, while some may say, as Aquinas points out in his first objection on this topic, that the borrower is consenting to the sin of the usurer when borrowing at interest, this misrepresents the relationship between the borrower and the lender. In our bizarro world of ballooning debt-laden economics, we can tend to forget the obvious and primary reason someone takes out a loan, which is, of course, because they need the money for something they otherwise could not have. The borrower is typically in a position of need, and the lender is typically someone in a position of means. It's not as if the borrower desires the usury that comes with the loan, as I am sure if given the option, the borrower would prefer the loan without the usury, but rather the borrower needs the money. This is not as if two equal parties consent to a sin, but rather the usurer takes advantage of the situation when another is in a position of need. The borrower is a victim of usury, and the victim of the sin of another is not guilty of sin. Or as Aquinas puts it: "He that suffers injury does not sin, according to the Philosopher, wherefore justice is not a mean between two vices, as stated in the same book. Now a usurer sins by doing an injury to the person who borrows from him under a condition of usury. Therefore he that accepts a loan under a condition of usury does not sin."[121] So, provided the borrower needs the money for a good cause, which I will leave for others to debate what constitutes a good reason to *borrow* money, the borrower does not sin if he takes a loan out at usury.

Another common retort I find, especially if my interlocutor has had a few beers before engaging in the discussion, is for someone to shake their fist in the air and ask incredulously - "What do you suppose we do without interest!? Do you just want us to be a bunch of communists!? Is that what you want!?" The argument is not typically well framed, but simply calling someone a communist does prove to be quite effective, so I will go ahead and say directly that the scope of this argument has nothing to do for or against communism, socialism, or the free-market system itself. I argue that

---

[120] *English Standard Version.*
[121] *New Advent*, Aquinas, *Summa Theologia*, Second Part of the Second Part, Question 78, Article 4, https://www.newadvent.org/summa/3078.htm

lending at interest is a sin, and I often point out the absurdity of our *monetary* system in hopes of making this argument compelling; however, I intend to say nothing in this book about the *economic* system itself.

Along those same lines of what may be obvious, but I would rather just say it directly lest it be assumed incorrectly, I am not arguing against profit or business partnerships. Nothing is wrong with a business being profitable - justly profitable endeavors are wonderful. Additionally, there is nothing wrong with people partnering in different ways in these business endeavors. These *societas,* as they were known in Roman law, were accepted as licit throughout the scholastic debates on usury, and I see whatever questions may exist around business partnerships today to be a separate question to that of usury.

In my experience discussing usury with a wide range of folks with varying interests in the topic and from many different theological and philosophical backgrounds, one common theme, among others, has emerged, especially from Christians who hold what I would call traditional or orthodox beliefs in most matters of the faith. These folks are often rather troubled when they are shown the evidence from scripture and struggle to find an obvious way to reconcile scripture with our general acceptance of lending at interest, so they will then begin asking probing questions to make sense of the matter. These questions are like the ones we discussed above, such as whether interest should be justified because of inflation, opportunity cost, business loans, or other exceptions. Eventually, the inquisitor will find an exception in some obscure situation that sounds compelling. "So, you're telling me that my sweet, sweet, great aunt, Betty Sue, is a usurer? My sweet Betty Sue, whose husband built their little ranch home after World War II with his bare hands, and is now selling this home to her niece below market value and is only asking for 1.5% interest on the seller-financed sale because Betty Sue likes to have a Little Debbie cake every afternoon with a glass of tea when she watches *Wheel of Fortune.* She has noticed that these cakes keep getting more expensive, and she wants to have enough money each month to cover the extra cost. Are you saying this Betty Sue is a usurer? My Betty Sue? There's just no way." With the inquisitor convinced, perhaps justifiably so, that his sweet Betty Sue is not a usurer, and having found one obscure exception to assuage his conscience, he can now put the whole thing to rest without giving a second thought to the avalanche of other situations that surround him that do not fit this exception pattern. To the inquisitor, Betty Sue's atypical situation quickly becomes conflated with the most extreme, calculated, and ruthless actions you could imagine from the Federal Reserve, and all concerns over usury are forgotten. In minutes, the inquisitor followed the same path Christendom followed over the last several centuries. Obscure exceptions for why usury did not apply in certain situations were valiantly fought for. Once these skirmishes were won, they were conflated with the entire war, and soon all could be forgotten. Whether it logically made sense that these exceptions could apply at scale did not seem to matter, as the inquisitor in the individual situation and society at large had both found the justification for usury that their hearts desired.

In summary, considering these different exceptions or extrinsic titles then and now, I find most of them fall short, and the ones that do not fall short, I suspect, would only apply in rare and narrow circumstances today. I still believe the best definition of usury is the simple one that prevailed throughout the majority of the Christian faith - usury is receiving more from a loan of money or other fungible items than what is lent. It does seem that *damnum emergens* (accrued damages) or covering for inflation would be appropriate reasons to charge additional money to *break even* when factoring in these considerations; however, these should never justify making a profit above and beyond the additional impact of these extrinsic titles. All other titles or exceptions, such as lucrum cessans (opportunity cost), periculum sortis (risk), or business loans should be rejected. When these rules are applied, I think you would find that the vast majority of the lending activity that exists today should be considered usury and, therefore, sinful.

5. Where Do We Go from Here?

"The Christian ideal has not been tried and found wanting. It has been found difficult; and left untried." - G.K. Chesterton[122]

If you have made it this far and are at least open to the idea of seeing usury in a different light than the modern norm, I suspect you may be wondering, "What do we do with this information?" For those expecting a neat, tidy, and practical answer to resolving this mess, I will warn you from the outset that I will not deliver what you desire. I believe the challenges we face in the present moment relating to usury make practical discernment especially difficult when considering both systemic contexts and individual demands to live out a life of holiness. And yet, while the journey to the heavenly kingdom as it relates to usury will be long and uncertain, I do pray some take this journey, even if it's just a timid, clumsy, first step in the dark in faith.

I have alluded to several common objections I encounter to the idea that usury is a sin throughout the book, and there is one final objection I have yet to mention. On the *Pilgrim's Progress* to seeing what I believe to be the truth about usury, many are diverted at early steps in their journey by the "Worldly Wise Man" who speaks so eloquently on economics or by a stroll through "Vanity Fair" where they see all the beautiful things you can buy with someone else's labors. Still, some make it almost there and see through our economic system's shams and the unavoidable biblical truth about usury. Yet, when they reach the end and face what should be done with this uncomfortable truth, they throw up their hands and forget the whole thing. Although they do not state their logic for this directly, they seem to believe "this problem seems hard to tackle, and therefore, there must not be a problem." Perhaps for some, this is a marker of wisdom - there are countless problems we hear of daily that are well beyond our capacity to solve. It would be foolish and show a rather arrogant lack of faith to think each of us needs to step into all of them. And yet, while it may be true that not *all* of us are called to wrestle with our usury situation, *some* of us certainly are. If it is indeed true that entire generations have completely ignored or scoffed at important biblical truths, how can that not spur Christians to action? While the answers on what should be done

---

[122] G. K. Chesterton, *What's Wrong with the World.*

with the truth of usury remain far from certain to me, I pray for the faith and courage not to let go as I wrestle with these inconvenient truths, and if my hip falls out of joint in the struggle, so be it. For any who would like to join this fight, I will offer you the best I can now, even if all I can provide is a glimpse into the various intellectual grapplings I have had the last several years on what can or should be done from a practical perspective relating to usury. Perhaps another book will be written with clearer steps to combat the sin of usury systemically and within our individual lives. Hopefully, that book will come from a smarter and better writer than me. Still, in the meantime, I will share the furthest I have been able to progress in my thinking as it relates to the systemic challenges of combating usury, the opportunities and challenges to living a life of personal holiness relating to usury, and how the reality of our situation can bring an even deeper appreciation for our desperate need for Christ.

Part 1: Navigating the Systemic Challenges with Usury

Regarding navigating the systemic challenges associated with usury, I see no benefit in sugarcoating the situation - we have gotten ourselves into quite the pickle. God's harshest judgment is often to give us exactly what we desire. As C. S. Lewis puts it in *The Great Divorce*, "There are only two kinds of people in the end: those who say to God, 'Thy will be done,' and those to whom God says, in the end, 'Thy will be done.'"[123] Or as Paul says in Romans, "And since they did not see fit to acknowledge God, God gave them up to a debased mind to do what ought not to be done."[124] Such is our state of affairs with money - we have long ignored God in matters of money, and it seems as if God has given us over to our absurd lusts and the resulting consequences with this system we have created.

To put our primary problem quite bluntly, we have created a global avalanche of debt, creating seemingly impossible situations for us to try and navigate. Modern money is debt, and each time money is created, it comes in the form of a debt arrangement where the borrower owes more money than what was created by the debt arrangement. If I borrow $100 and owe $110, the loan creates $100, but I still owe $10 greater than what was created, and therefore, for the $10 to be repaid, there must either be another loan to create

[123] C. S. Lewis, *The Great Divorce* (New York: HarperOne, 2009), 75.
[124] Romans 1:28.

more money in the system or the borrower must exchange their labor or resources to extinguish the debt. Rarely are the debts, especially in aggregate, paid back while they are small and manageable, so typically someone else takes out a loan that creates $10, that would also come with an expectation to pay more than the loan itself. So, if that $10 loan is made, it would come with the expectation to pay $11, so now we are even worse off as the collective system is now $11 short ($110 created with $121 owed)! To pay off the $11 loan, more money will typically be created, which is just more debt, which will require an even greater repayment. I think you probably get the point by now: in a system such as this, debt and consumption must either grow perpetually and exponentially, or else the entire system collapses.

Several peculiar economic orthodoxies were taught throughout our lives that never fully made sense to me until I realized our system is a giant pyramid of debt. One such orthodoxy is the prevailing wisdom around inflation. We strive for the Goldilocks amount of inflation - too much inflation and money will be deemed worthless, and anarchy will ensue, too little inflation and growth will not be great enough, but worst of all would be deflation as that could threaten the whole thing. But if inflation means things get more expensive and deflation means things get cheaper, then would we not want and expect deflation? If humanity is on the one-way escalator of progress like so many of us unreflectively assume, should things not become cheaper as we become more productive and efficient? In a system with a stable money supply, deflation would result as we produce more - but that is not our system. We want gradual inflation brought about by increasing debt and gradual growth brought about by corresponding levels of increasing consumption and production as this offers the greatest chance for the system to continue for another year. If the new base of debt is not larger than the previous base, then the system risks becoming inverted and imploding upon itself.

This is why we dread a recession so much. A recession is nothing more than two consecutive quarters where we produce less than we previously did. Think about how much we produce and waste on any given day - should a little less production be that big of a deal? In the absence of mountains of debt, we could consciously choose to produce less and could probably all benefit from doing so, and yet in our current system, a word such as "recession" that simply means "less production" sends shivers up our spines.

Some of the great saints speak of the bondage of our will, where we are like addicts to sin and are incapable of not sinning. With the captive nature of sin, you willfully surrender your volition and choose to be no longer able to choose other than to sin until the grace of God transforms your heart. Such is the state of our corporate sin with money as well. While the sins of usury and fraudulent fractional reserve lending that created this mess were probably driven by greed and pride and a combination of other sins, in our current state, greed is not even necessary to continue to drive the perpetual growth and consumption of our world - we hardly have a choice in the matter. If every iota of greed left every human heart instantaneously, little would change in the short term regarding the state of our economic affairs. Money in its current form demands growth - it would cease to exist without perpetual growth, and we have ceded most of the decision-making authority in the world to the pursuit of whatever money deems necessary to keep itself afloat.

Our monetary Pharoah can take away our straw and demand just as many bricks, chastising the laziness of any who cannot keep up with quotas, and there's nothing we can do about it. In a debt-based system, money is a zero-sum affair - for every credit, there must be a corresponding debt, so if all the debts were paid off, then money would cease to exist. Except, our system is a less-than-zero-sum system because we are a debt-based system with the expectation of usury, such that more money is owed at any given time than money that exists in the system. Therefore, the survival of the system precludes the possibility for *everyone* to pay off their debts - only some can.

Imagine ten families are captured and locked in a room by some twisted game master who tells the families that he will only feed nine of them, and they must decide among themselves who gets fed. After making the gut-wrenching decision on who will be left out, the nine are fed, and the one family eventually dies off. Still, after a while, the game master returns and tells the remaining nine families that only seven of them will be fed. So, they decide which two will be left out, and those two families eventually die off. Later, the game master returns and tells the seven families that only four will be fed. Imagine the temptations of these captives to treat each other ruthlessly out of concern for self-preservation. Such is our condition. We all have debts, and not all of us can pay them. We are in a less than zero-sum game such that the entire system would implode before the debt payoffs were close to complete.

While this may all sound bleak, part of the reason I want to paint the picture this way, besides the fact that I think it to be accurate, is that I do not think we pause enough to admit the horrendous situation so many of us are in, and failing to acknowledge our situation just makes matters worse. We are so often reminded about how we are the richest people in the history of the world, which is probably true in many respects as it relates to the amount of stuff and technology we have available to us, but we are often directly or indirectly shamed into feeling guilty about this "wealth." Perhaps much of that is justified - many of us are complicit in this system in complex ways - but most of us are not really that wealthy, as we hardly *own* anything of value. Even for those who do possess true ownership of some assets, most of those things that we do own are typically only valuable insofar as our economic systems continue in their current form.

And for every person who can claim ownership in this system, there are many more of us, and even many of those in the middle and upper-middle classes, who are anxiously trying to stay afloat with our debt payments one month at a time. While *some* of us may be perpetrators of injustice in matters of usury and debt, we are almost *all* victims of this injustice. And while it's horrible enough to be stuck in an abusive relationship that you are powerless to remove yourself from, it's even worse if you are made to feel guilty about the abuse being inflicted upon you.

For everyone in the world with either a mortgage or rent to pay, which is certainly a huge portion of us, you are under the constant threat of exile from your community with circumstances that are largely out of your control. Sure, you can make yourself as valuable as possible to your organization or create business opportunities to minimize the chances that you are the one to lose your income which could lead to exile, and sure you can diligently save to minimize these risks, but this is not a universally viable strategy in our current system. When you do this, you are not outrunning the lion; you are just outrunning your neighbor whom the lion devours. While someone who advises you to avoid debt and to live as frugally as possible may give great personal financial advice that will benefit certain individuals, our economic system would likely implode before all the debt could even be repaid if a critical mass of individuals were able to live out this type of advice. The United States is over

$34,750,000,000,000 in debt as of the time of writing, and while it is tragically comical to hear politicians blame one another for the problem and promise that their respective sides will help with the matter, none of them can do anything about it as to repay even a critical mass of the debt would implode the system.

As the system becomes more unsustainable with increasingly absurd growth expectations, monetary growth reaches its tentacles into every dark crevasse of uncaptured territory. With the colossal pressure of debt bearing down on the world, everyone scrambles to turn whatever they can into money to keep afloat. When everything we can imagine must turn into money, we end up with a tragic King Midas situation. We initially rejoice at our power to conjure money with one keyboard stroke. However, we weep when our golden touch withers our food supply and turns even our most cherished relationships into nothing but lifeless statues. We lust after money, transferring more and more of our time into activities that make money, and we are not even shy about the language we use to describe this. Something can only become a vocation if it can be "monetized." And yet, money is but a sign - it points to something else. Just as the moon reflects the sun and produces no light by itself, money reflects the value of the goods it represents, but by itself, it produces no value. If you forget the source of the light and chase only its reflection, the light will die. Just as our prideful hearts curve inwardly on themselves and worship our own reflected light, while the true light within us becomes dimmer and dimmer until it's but a speck beyond recognition, our lust for money curves us inwardly on ourselves in a similar manner. As we monetize everything, we forget that money represents other things and is not a true good. As the true value of money wanes, we cling even more desperately to money itself, not the things it represents, which just exacerbates the problem by weakening money further. And yet, all the while, money loses its luster; we devote more and more attention to it.

So, as I hope you now see, we find ourselves in quite a precarious situation, but before we get into what could or could not be done about our situation, I want to pause to state a few things, lest I be misunderstood. As hopeless as this sounds to be surrounded and confined by such ubiquitous evil, please do not misunderstand me to think that I am saying that all that has happened and will continue to happen within this system is for naught. What others meant for evil, "God meant it for good."[125] Much good has happened through the mess of this system, and these good things are truly good. All the great technological inventions, the wonderful advancements in modern medicine, and all the beautiful things that have been accomplished in recent decades and centuries are still good things. While I do not think the good of these things justifies the sins of usury as the ends do not justify the means, I also do not believe the fruit of the poisonous tree applies such that all that has been accomplished within a corrupt system, and even at times spurred along because of the corruption of the system, diminishes the greatness of those works.

And while some have had the privilege to contribute to great works on this earth, all is not lost, even for those of us forced to endure mundane or cruel work under misguided direction with hardly anything tangible to notice for our efforts. God has undoubtedly used these opportunities for those souls who seek Him for their sanctification and the sanctification of others. The history of the world is littered with times when people are forced to operate under cruel regimes with forced labor to achieve misguided objectives, and this era certainly has its manifestations of these conditions. Their work is still not without purpose for those suffering in these conditions, even if a discernible material benefit cannot be identified. The physical effects of most work under even the most virtuous of regimes will be forgotten and discarded in the blink of an eye. Still, diligent work's impact on immortal souls will last forever, regardless of the corruption it was forced to endure.

There is one last item I want to address in this space before moving on. As I consider mundane or cruel work in the sections above, I mostly have in mind monotonous, underpaid work that threatens to sap the vitality from one's soul, but does not rise to the level of being torturously cruel or physically unsafe. For anyone reading this who happens to be enduring cruelty of a greater magnitude, I would not want the above considerations to appear flippant. While anything I write may just be cold comfort in this type of situation, I do know that God hears the groanings of those in these conditions especially, and just as God heard the groaning from the Israelites in Egypt (Exodus 2:23-24) and ultimately delivered them from their conditions, God hears the groanings of all the oppressed today and will eventually bring deliverance for those who seek Him, whether in

---

[125] Genesis 50:20. *English Standard Version.*

this life or the next. A God who sees you (Genesis 16:13) reigns sovereign over every square inch of His creation, and this same God will bring justice for all. Those who perpetrate these especially wicked types of cruelty without repentance will have no place to hide (Revelation 20:11).

Part 2: False Pseudo Solutions

You may be thinking, "It is all fine and dandy that some good can be accomplished through this mess, but when will you talk about how to fix the problem in the first place?" I suppose now is as good a time as any to try and tackle this question head-on; however, as I warned in an earlier chapter, sometimes "the longest way round is the shortest way home,"[126] and I think that is ultimately what applies here as well. While I desperately hope I am wrong with this next statement, I just cannot envision how things do not get worse before they get better with this predicament we have created. These types of situations do not typically have graceful landings; rather, they result in heartbreak, shame, and fractured relationships across society. Most of our modern world has been built upon one big lie - a representation of reality different than it truly is, and whenever the truth finally crashes through this big lie, it will probably be painful at first. That is not to say hope is lost, as nothing could be further from the truth. "The arc of the moral universe is long, but it bends toward justice."[127] God is all-powerful, all-good, all-knowing, and all-wise, and love eventually wins. The heavenly economy is one of love, each willing the good of the other and building mutual trust and reciprocal benefit for the common good through the process, and this kingdom will eventually prevail. While I plead that it will be "on earth as it is in heaven"[128] quite soon, we have quite a way to go until this is the norm in our earthly life.

My corporate career has mostly consisted of assessing business problems using the tried and true "people, process, and technology" framework. While technology and process problems undoubtedly exist, I typically find that if you press hard enough, people problems are usually at the root of the other problems. I find this situation with our monetary system to be no different. Many who hold similar

---

[126] Lewis, *Mere Christianity*, 87.
[127] Martin Luther King, Jr., "Remaining Awake Through a Great Revolution," *Oberlin College Archives*,
https://www2.oberlin.edu/external/EOG/BlackHistoryMonth/MLK/CommAddress.html
[128] Matthew 6:10.

views regarding the evils of the central banking system are quick to propose technology or process solutions to our predicaments. Many will tout a return to a true gold standard or the widespread adoption of a blockchain ledger system to remedy our ails, and in many ways, I agree with some of these arguments. A serious problem of our current system is that there's no limit to the amount of money that can be created, and history has shown that whoever holds this god-like power to create money can rarely maintain virtuous restraint in doing so. Suppose everyone can just agree that monetary creation should be limited by the natural supply of something like gold, or a cryptocurrency solution where the amount of money is capped by the design of the system. In that case, you can at least stop the problems that come from the unfettered explosion of money into a system. And while there must eventually be some process change in our system as even a universal and immediate repentance from everyone in the world would not alone solve our problems, I do not believe a system or process change without sincere repentance will do much good either. Even if we have prophetic powers to "understand all mysteries and all knowledge"[129] as it relates to matters of money, "but have not love, then we are nothing."[130]

Suppose the primary motivator for much of society is to accrue as much money as possible, simply to accrue money and not as a means to another objective. In that case, you will have this constant "king of the hill" type jockeying to the top regarding either being able to produce or acquire money. If our hearts remain unchanged, then monetary reform will not be in pursuit of justice; rather, it will just be one tyranny overthrowing another one.

Whereas currently, those at the top of the hill have created a scheme where they can just type numbers into a computer to control the actions of much of the world, if this desire to accrue money reigns paramount, the shrewd and the strong will find a way to acquire and exploit this power regardless of the system. We can just look at history to see how this plays out with the gold standard. The physically strong nations will conquer, rape, and pillage for gold, and the intellectually strong will defraud their customers through fractional reserve lending, even though these both just result in inflation.[131] It seems naive to think that returning to the gold

---

[129] 1 Corinthians 13:2.

[130] 1 Corinthians 13:2.

[131] Niall Furguson, *The Ascent of Money: A Financial History of the World: 10th Anniversary Edition* (New York: Penguin Books, 2009), Chapter 1.

standard alone will resolve our problems. We just came from there - that would be the textbook definition of insanity to do the same thing and expect a different result. The gold standard led to receipt currency, which led to fractional lending, fractional lending led to central banks, and central banks eventually led to purely fiat debt-based currency. If usury remains a benign impetus to the economy in the minds of most of the world, then why would we expect this to end differently this time?

Yet others will say that progress is our future, that all we need to do is embrace cryptocurrency, and that all will be solved. I have even started seeing television commercials at the time of this writing essentially saying this same thing. The system is a mess, but cryptocurrency will save the system, and our futures will all be grand. Now my goal here is not to bash cryptocurrency as I do not think I am sufficiently educated on the topic to suggest what role it should play in an economy fully; however, I do strongly believe that a shift to cryptocurrency *without* repentance will inevitably lead us with similar problems manifesting themselves in different ways. Virtuous people will reform a corrupt system, but corrupt people will inevitably find ways to exploit even the most thoughtful systems. And suffice it to say we are miles from virtue in money matters.

As I understand it, cryptocurrency systems are like distributed ledgers in extremely large locations. So currently, our economy is like one big pseudo-centralized ledger with the banks maintaining the ledger and reconciling all the transactions between individuals to derive the amount of money each individual has. With cryptocurrency systems, millions of individual computers each have a copy of the ledger that keeps track of our interactions with one another and the amount of currency everyone has. So instead of the banks being responsible for maintaining systemic trust in the accuracy of the ledger, systemic trust in the accuracy of the distributed ledgers would be maintained through complex cryptographic formulas and extremely powerful computing processing where these ledgers can keep a complete account of all transactions and can prevent individuals from fraudulently overriding transactions to misrepresent the amount of currency they have. Assuming these cryptocurrency systems can truly maintain accurate and almost fraudulent proof ledgers as well as they claim, which for the sake of argument I will assume they can, then one can rather easily imagine some serious benefits to a system that can provide banking-type services such as electronic payments and safe storage of currency without the need of the banking system itself as we know it today. And while this type of system would present new practical problems such as the sheer volume of energy and computing power that must be used and maintained as this scaled, or the risk of someone being locked out of their cryptocurrency accounts and losing hordes of wealth due to a simple oversight, I have no doubt the ingenuity of humans could figure out things such as this. So, at this point, I am not trying to argue either for or against the *practicality* of a cryptocurrency system as it relates to allowing the efficient and trusted exchange of money, but what I am saying is that if we just redirect our monetary lusts from fiat money to cryptocurrencies we will end up in a bad spot as our hearts are so desperately attached to money beyond our wildest comprehension. Without repentance, our lustful urges will continue to bulldoze whatever measly constraints a gold standard or a cryptocurrency system puts in our way of allowing money to maintain its rule over us.

Time may only tell the specific negative ways our idolatry will play out if we end up with a primarily cryptocurrency system without corresponding repentance. Still, there are some ways I think we can envision where problems will arise. Imagine for a moment that you had three different kings where the first king and some of his nobles have almost all the yellow beads in the world, the second king and some of his nobles have almost all the green beads in the world, and the third king and some of his nobles have almost all the red beads in the world. The kings all know that their subjects are clamoring for a system to facilitate easy trading among one another, so they just want the kings to decide on one color to use. While some have a few beads of various colors, most hardly have any, so they do not care which color they choose. However, the kings and the nobles have almost everything at stake because they could go from basically ruling the entire world to having almost no power whatsoever depending on where this seemingly arbitrary decision lands on whether to use red, yellow, or green beads. In this scenario, to what lengths could you imagine power-hungry kings and nobles going to ensure that their color beads are chosen or that they are shrewd enough to end up with a bounty of beads for whichever color is eventually chosen? Are we not seeing the early stages of something similar with the valuations of cryptocurrencies in their infancy? As the hordes throng back and forth from one cryptocurrency to another, their valuations, which are nothing more than the collective perception of how likely someone else will eventually want to trade goods and services for their currency, vacillate wildly. At this stage in the game, this can all seem rather harmless as most of us are on the periphery watching this happen, and for those who do have skin in the game, they are typically only investing a subset of their net worth; however, imagine the frenzy this would cause if cryptocurrency systems were the primary monetary systems in the world and therefore these obscene fluctuations in value represented the bulk of most of the world's wealth. One person could work and save their entire life and have their wealth evaporate overnight simply because the common consensus shifted from one cryptocurrency to another. Now, if we do go the cryptocurrency route as a society, I suspect there would be periods such as these of wild fluctuations. Eventually though, the populace would clamor for one ruling currency, and they would not even care which it was - they would just want someone to come in and bring some stability to the situation, no matter the cost. If this situation occurred, I suspect someone would step up to bring about this new Pax Romana, but it would come with serious costs.

But before that situation could even occur, another substantial roadblock must be sorted through before we could ever shift to cryptocurrency at scale anyway. That same challenge also offers a great segue into one of the other common pseudo-solutions discussed to our current predicament. Our current situation is a debt-based economy - the entire thing runs because people owe things to different people, and these debts are meticulously maintained by the folks in the banking system. But you can't shift from a debt-based system to a currency system without something being done with the debts - the debts must either be paid, forgiven, or carried forward to the new system. Within the Mosaic Law detailed in Deuteronomy and Leviticus, God instructs the Israelites to have debt forgiveness systems baked into their society. You also have Jesus Himself commanding us to ask for forgiveness of our debts "as we also have forgiven our debtors,"[132] so by and large, debt forgiveness seems like the way to go. However, in our modern society, the system is typically favored towards the creditor as opposed to the debtor, and even the recent shift towards some debt forgiveness programs by the government is more of a facade than true debt forgiveness. Part of the reason I think this to be the case goes back to the peculiar pyramid shape of our economy.

---

[132] Matthew 6:12.

Debt forgiveness is a rather simple concept in uncomplicated situations with two parties. Imagine I borrow $500 from a friend to pay my monthly rent, and I am indebted to my friend for $500. If my friend chooses to "forgive" my debt, where I am no longer obligated to pay him the $500, he would bear the full brunt of the cost. I could also do work for someone, and they may agree to pay me $100. However, they could fall on hard times and be unable to pay me. If I choose to "forgive" this debt, the other person would no longer owe me $100, and I would bear the brunt of the cost of this forgiveness. However, other situations will also be called debt forgiveness that are quite different when more than two parties are involved in the transaction. Imagine a ruler comes into power in a certain territory and discovers numerous debt arrangements already in place when he comes to power. The ruler could come in and declare that the debts are forgiven so that the debtors no longer owe the creditors their money. In this situation, though, the ruler is not bearing the cost of the forgiveness - the ruler is using his power to force the creditors to bear the brunt of the forgiveness. Now this could very well be a step in the direction of justice depending on the context of the situation, but this could also simply be a shrewd political move to curry favor with the debtor class.

The second situation is closer to what we have seen over the past few years with the resurgence of political rhetoric around forgiving student debt, except our peculiar economy makes this arrangement even further from true debt forgiveness. Now, my goal is not to make a stand either for or against these actions, but I do not want people to be misled into thinking that this form of debt forgiveness is the type of scalable solution to our ails. With student debt, you have at least three parties - you have the student who takes out a loan, you have the unholy trinity of the government and the banking system, which conjures the money that will be provided to the student, and you have the university which receives payment from the student. With debt forgiveness with only two parties, the one who forgives the debt is also the one who bears the cost for the forgiveness. In the student loan example, the student with her debt forgiven benefits greatly in this scenario. The college that provided the services to the student who has already received the money from the student is not obligated to pay the money back so that they would be mostly indifferent to the outcome. But who bears the brunt of the costs of this program? The debt that is forgiven is money that the government, commercial, and central banking trinity created out of nothing, and they can just create new money whenever they want, provided there is someone ready to accept their loans, so there is not any substantial burden that is borne by them. So, who pays for all of this? Just like many things, the general populace will pay for them through inflation, which necessarily results in prices rising when new money is constantly injected into the system.[133]

Now, perhaps that is the appropriate action that should be taken - I can imagine good faith arguments suggesting that the public should pay for the release from the crushing weight of debt for certain individuals - however, I do not want anyone to be deceived into thinking these band-aids are going to cure this raging cancer within our system ravaging our organs at breakneck speed. With debt forgiveness instructed by God to the Israelites, this debt forgiveness is just one part of a comprehensive social system with other relational and authoritative bonds such that true debt forgiveness can occur without unfettering all social bonds. Even in situations that have occurred throughout history separate from the Israelite example where a new ruler comes in and abolishes existing debts, presumably, the new ruler would have systems in mind to take the place of the function that the debts were performing in binding society together. However, in our modern system, debt *is* the system, and ultimately, the relational and authoritative bonds at a systemic level are subservient to the debt, so the only way that debt can truly be forgiven at scale is if the entire system as we know it ceases to exist.

Suppose we go back to the cryptocurrency idea and imagine how we may end up switching to cryptocurrency as our primary system within the world or in certain economies. In that case, I suspect this will be a bumpy transition as individuals still owe money in dollars, pesos, or whatever currency they use. Since substantial forgiveness of these debts cannot occur without ending the system as we know it, anytime current debts are paid in the current system they necessarily are replaced with new debts (remember the creation of money needed to pay off current debts comes with debt greater than the creation of new money added to the system), then the only other option would be for the debts to somehow transition to the new cryptocurrency system, which effectively leaves most people in the same system, just under a different name.

In summary, we are naive if we believe that shifting to a gold

---

[133] Marc Barnes and Jacob Iman, hosts, "Student Loan Forgiveness." *Good Money,* 11 October 2022, https://newpolity.com/podcasts-hub/student-loans

standard or a cryptocurrency system will alone resolve the problems we have created due to the exponentially growing debt at the core of our system. For starters, the debt that drives the system cannot be easily relinquished as that would abolish it. The complex web of debt and debtor relationships that make up the system itself is basically what most of the known world has relied upon for their entire lives to mediate societal relationships and bonds. So, when we talk about debt forgiveness nowadays, we are not talking about truly forgiving the debt in the system. Therefore, any new system we shift to would transfer the same debt obligations as the current system unless we resolve the debt problem. And even if we do resolve the debt challenge and shift to a new system, if our hearts are hell-bent on accumulating money no matter the cost, the strong and the shrewd will continue to find ways to exploit whatever new system we come up with, unless we have substantial repentance such that enough individuals can articulate and seek out true justice to counteract rule stemming from the unjust acquisition of money.

Now, I know it may seem as if I am being negative about there being any hope to resolve this, but that is only partially my intent. This *will* eventually be resolved. Good has already won the war - the skirmishes between good and evil still occurring in this lifetime are just there to allow time until everyone has had sufficient opportunity to switch to the right side before the ultimate terms of the peace treaty are enacted. The reason I have laid out challenges to each of the systemic pseudo-solutions is not intended to be discouraging as a whole. Still, it is intended to discourage us from trying to solve these problems through *only* our fallen intellect and prideful ambitions without first kneeling in humility and seeking counsel from the only source who can lead us to true justice in these matters. "Watch out that no one deceives you. For many will come in my name, claiming, 'I am the Messiah,' and will deceive many."[134] We should beware of placing our hopes in a fully secular solution to solve the problems of nearly ubiquitous sin related to money. This is the main problem as I see it - our hearts have gone astray. While we may have many other problems related to usury, nothing can be done without first addressing the condition of our hearts.

Part 3: On Christ the Solid Rock I Stand

For those still with me, you probably realize I will not be your source

---

[134] Matthew 24:4-5.

for a systemic solution to this mess. However, you may be experiencing a tinge of conviction at these ideas and still wondering, "What does it mean to maintain personal holiness relating to usury and the idolatry of money in light of the inherent challenges thrust upon us by our current systems?" Again, my answers will probably disappoint anyone looking for crystal clear clarity on this question, as I still often wonder about this myself. Still, I will share what I can, hoping it will be beneficial.

In one sense the answer is obvious - if lending at interest is a sin, then simply do not lend at interest. This piece seems to me to be manageable as it just means that if you lend money directly (which few of us typically do anyway), you should not charge interest on the loan. If you deposit money in the bank, you should not receive interest on your deposits as these are basically like loans, and you should not have investments in bonds as these are just interest-bearing loans. If someone wanted to get technical on these areas, perhaps you could justify some of them with the inflation argument, provided you are truly not seeking a profit, but rather are only looking to be made even after inflation. Still, I would be wary of using these exceptions as they could just be an excuse to sin.

And while these types of actions may come close to exhausting the expectations of the literal letter of the law as it relates to avoiding being a usurer, they just scratch the surface of what may be expected of us as it relates to avoiding the idolatry of money. People in Christian circles talk often about the dangers of the love of money, and while these are wise warnings, I think even those who preach these things typically do not fully understand just how deep the roots of our idolatry run. When people warn of the love of money, they typically consider the dangers of pursuing money at the expense of other more important relationships, which is quite a serious concern. However, our reality is much worse than this, as even those who establish the strictest limits of moderation in the pursuit of money and exercise the most charitable giving cannot escape the idolatry that lies with the ontology and sustainment of modern money that none of us can escape. At any given moment, billions of people worldwide disregard reason, logic, and love in favor of faith in money. This is the air we breathe. This is the water in which we swim. This system we have is an antichrist system in the sense that its principles are the antithesis of the principles of Christ. God is love, and love wills the good of the other even at the expense of self, whereas modern money is parasitic and consumes the other for its own sake. And yet, despite this, when faced with obvious evidence from the Bible or church tradition suggesting that usury is a sin, most of those claiming devotion to Christ instead defend our antichrist economic system. The answer to our problems is not some new technology or process, but rather, it is the same answer that Jesus proclaimed thousands of years ago - "repent and believe in the gospel."[135]

But even if one is willing to condemn the sin as it relates to this system wholeheartedly, how are we to be in the world but not of the world as it relates to usury? While the inner workings of a repentant turn towards God brought about by His grace may forever remain mysterious to me, the actions that a repentant heart takes are often quite clear. How a miser turns towards generosity and why some misers remain that way and others do not, I may never know, but the fact that sharing your wealth with others signifies a repentant heart, whereas clutching your wealth all to yourself does not, is obvious. However, I find our situation with repentance and usury much more complex, as our entire system is based upon usury. How are we to be in the world but not of the world as it relates to this?

For just one practical example, how should one ethically feel if they are not directly practicing usury but work for someone who practices usury, and therefore, receive their wages from a usurer? For those feeling overconfident at this first question because they do not work for a bank, what if you work for a company that makes some of their money through interest, even though that is not their core business model? The big companies that so many of us work for are massive, and it often takes years within an organization to truly figure out all the different ways they make money. It's not uncommon that buried within a company's business processes will be some way that they profit through usury. And even for those who could say that they do not work for a company that profits through usury directly, how many industries are propped up indirectly by usury and debt at the system's core? How many funds received by companies are primarily the result of someone else being burdened by debt so they have enough money to purchase a particular product? How much of the growth pursued by business owners is truly in the best interest of their employees, customers, and other stakeholders rather than an unfortunate necessity imposed by the ever-increasing debt of the

---

[135] Mark 1:14.

system or a prideful urge to win simply for the sake of winning in a situation where competition was an unnecessary way to view the situation? How does one discern right from wrong when navigating a world marred with such pervasive evil where there are often no pure choices? Knowing that cowardice can masquerade itself as prudence, while foolishness can just as easily masquerade as bravery, I remain in tension while sorting out how to live a life of personal holiness through God's grace while trying to support a family in this financially messed up world in which we live.[136] Of course, I know the ultimate Provider is the real support as the primary cause all along the way. Still, as I fumble through this world as a secondary cause, I am far from confident in my discernment of how to earn a living ethically.

And yet, this uncertainty should not leave any of us in despair. Quite the opposite! This should bring us back to an even greater appreciation of grace. God is sovereign over *all* these things, and through no merit of our own, God's grace will not stop until we are eventually molded into creatures capable of loving others as God loves us. We must not confuse His sovereignty as an excuse to be indifferent to sin, but we should rest confidently that His grace will encourage and mature our stumbles as we strive to live out His grace in money matters. As George MacDonald says, "God is easy to please, but hard to satisfy."[137] Christ's outburst at the moneychangers in the temple ought to frighten us from indifference; however, His repeatedly patient and grace filled approach with the disciples as they stumble should encourage us as we navigate these uncomfortable truths.

As Chesterton says, "The Christian ideal has not been tried and found wanting. It has been found difficult, and left untried."[138] I am not saying anything I have written should be easy to acknowledge or implement in this lifetime for any of us. However, if our current path dooms us to certain destruction, we ought not to resign ourselves to this state just because the way out is at times unclear. A chance at restoration is better than a certain doom.

---

[136] I would recommend researching Marc Barnes and Jacob Imam of NewPolity for anyone looking for great sources to engage in the practical questions of holiness regarding matters of money in our modern economy. I would also like to thank them for the work they have done in this space and the many thoughts within this book that have been spurred along by their Podcasts.

[137] Lewis, *Mere Christianity*, 203.

[138] Chesterton, *What's Wrong with the World*.

If this book has any impact on the reader, I hope it is this - that it will nudge you or shock you into reevaluating where you have built your house. I am more convinced than ever that we have built so many of our houses on sand, and these simply will not stand the coming floods. If a rebuild is in order, we must accept this disconcerting truth instead of adding more stories to mansions that will soon topple over. Suppose we have the faith and courage to see these things as they need to be seen. In that case, I have no doubt God will reveal the blueprints and direct the rebuilding efforts in whatever manner necessary, and the result will be more glorious than we could have ever dreamt up in our wildest dreams.